P9-CAG-237

Feminism for the Health of It

Wilma Scott Heide

Wilma Scott Heide was born on February 26, 1921 and died on May 8, 1985 of a heart attack. One of the most respected of feminist/human rights scholars/activists in the world, Dr. Heide was a nurse, sociologist, writer, activist and lecturer. During her lifetime she actively demonstrated intellectual force, caring and commitment in articulating the women's movement imperatives for society. She served as visiting professor and scholar at several universities, consultant to various state education associations and innumerable colleges, churches and many branches of the government, education and social organizations. In 1984 Wilma described herself as: *Behavioral Scientist at American Institutes for Research; Human Relations Commissioner in Pennsylvania; Chairone of Board and President of NOW (1970-1974); Professor of Women's studies and Public Affairs at Sangamon State (would-be) University in Illinois; Feminist and Humorist-at-Large.*

Feminism for the Health of It

Wilma Scott Heide

Foreword by

Jessie Bernard

Margaretdaughters, Inc.

Copyright © 1985 by Margaretdaughters, Inc.

All rights reserved. Inquiries should be addressed to:
Margaretdaughters, Inc.
P.O. Box 70
Buffalo, NY 14222

Book and cover design by Charlene Eldridge Wheeler

Printed in the United States of America

Library of Congress Cataloging-in-Publication Data

Heide, Wilma Scott, 1921-1985.
    Feminism for the health of it.

    Bibliography: p.
    Includes index.
    1. Feminism – United States. 2. Women – Health and hygiene –
United States – Sociological aspects. 3. Women in education – United
States. 4. Public welfare – United States. I. Title.
HQ1426.H45 1985   305.4′2′0973   85-15363
ISBN 0-931911-01-X (pbk.)

Grateful acknowledgement is made for permission to quote from the
following:
    Rita Arditti, "Women in Science: 'Women Drink Water While Men
Drink Wine'" *Science for the People*, Vol.VIII, No.2, March, 1976, pp.24-26.
    Portions of Chapter One previously appeared as "The Quest for Humanity Via
Higher Education," by Wilma Scott Heide, in *Learning Tomorrows: Commen-
tary on the Future of Education*, edited by Peter H. Wagshal, New York, Praeger
Publishers, 1979, pp.27-40.
    Portions of Chapter Two previously appeared as "Feminism: Making a
Difference in Our Health," by Wilma Scott Heide, in *The Woman Patient:
Medical and Psychological Interfaces, Vol.I: Sexual and Reproductive Aspects
of Women's Health Care*, edited by Malkah T. Notman, MD and Carol C.
Nadelson, MD, Plenum Press, New York, 1978, pp.9-19.
    Portions of Chapter Three previously appeared as "Scholarship/Action: In the
Human Interest," by Wilma Scott Heide, in *Signs: Journal of Women in Culture
and Society*, Vol.5, No.1, Autumn, 1979, pp.189-191.

TABLE OF CONTENTS

Foreword by Jessie Bernard   vii

Preface   xi

1 Quest for Our Humanity via Higher Education   1

2 Feminism: Making a Difference in Our Health   33

3 Scholarship: Action in the Human Interest   55

4 Economics: Breastimony on H.R. 9030 "Welfare Reform"   73

5 Future Search for Well-Fare   105

6 Communications: The Feminist Difference   117

7 Thinking the Thinkable: From Masculinism to Feminism   135

8 Women's World: International Politics   149

Index   160

Publisher's Note

Wilma Scott Heide died as this book was in preparation. She had completed reviewing and approving all of the edited manuscript, and had seen a facsimile of the cover incorporating the design she had suggested. Wilma loved the color yellow; she wanted this book cover to be in yellow and purple because these were the colors of the suffrage movement. She wore a silver pendant around her neck from which we designed the logo for the book; Wilma wanted the circle of the women's/peace symbol to reflect the globe. The adult and children figures were to represent "all people of the earth."

A few days before her death, Wilma discussed with us several matters that were still not completed. She was planning to add an open letter to the media; she intended to invite Jessie Bernard to write the foreword to the book. She indicated that she was giving thought to the acknowledgements, and reflected on how difficult it would be to adequately express her appreciation to the many people who had influenced her work. Although some of these details have been of necessity left undone, we have followed Wilma's guidance to the extent that is possible in completing the publication of this book. We know that she had many friends and loved ones to whom she wished to express her appreciation. To all readers whose path crossed Wilma's, to all who have contributed so generously to this work, you have helped to make this book possible; in her memory we extend to you our deep appreciation.

– Charlene Eldridge Wheeler and Peggy L. Chinn

Other titles available from Margaretdaughters:

Peace and Power: A Handbook of Feminist Process by Charlene Eldridge Wheeler and Peggy L. Chinn

A Feminist Legacy: The Ethics of Wilma Scott Heide and Company by Eleanor Humes Haney

FOREWORD

Who is the happy Warrior? Who is she
That every one in arms should wish to be?
It is the generous spirit ...
Whose high endeavors are an inward light
That makes the path before her always bright;
Who, with a natural instinct to discern
What knowledge can perform, is diligent to learn.[1]

Inappropriate as it may seem to apply the "warrior" figure of speech to a woman as opposed to war as Wilma Scott Heide was (Chapter 7), still she did seem to have the happy Warrior's "natural instinct to discern what knowledge" could do for women, and she was indeed "diligent to learn." The first chapter in this book is about the importance of knowledge. Not the limited male-created body of knowledge, but the new knowledge now being created by women. Wilma was also – like the godmother of her first profession Florence Nightingale – a "lady with a lamp." She was, that is, among the first cohort of women who participated in the Feminist Enlightenment beginning in the late 60s. To a growing number of women it was becoming clear that the first step toward their empowerment was active participation in the creation of knowledge. The great body of inherited human knowledge to date was a male achievement. It had been created by men, dealt with subjects that interested men, embodied almost exclusively the experience of men. When or if women were dealt with it was always from the point of view of their relations to men. Much of it was misogynist. Wilma saw it as a rape of women's minds (p.6). It was beinning to occur to many women that even their own image of themselves was based on male knowledge. Wilma decried a system of higher education based almost wholly on the transmission of this male-biased body of knowledge (pp.1-5). Her lamp carried oil to the torch of the Feminist Enlightenment that was rendering the female world visible, showing all the female experience that had been left out of the male canon.

Wilma was by temperament an activist first and foremost; but hers was always an activism solidly based on scholarship (Chapter 3). She read, she studied, she kept *au courant* – but always to shed light on basic feminist issues; on health (Chapter 2), on public welfare (Chapters 4,5), on communication (including language, the broadcast media, the print media, Chapter 6), and war (Chapter 7). She felt "ultimate optimism" (p.5) about success for the Feminist Enlightenment already beaming its light far and wide in:

> the increasingly serious and purposeful writings of women, women's studies programs, feminist presses, formal and informal communications networks, bookstores, infiltration of the library system and associations, multi-media creations, women's centers, professional and academic caucuses, countless conferences and much more learner-initiated re-socialization...Throughout this work, there is an intense commitment to the quality of human life rather than individual achievement of "success." (p.69)

It is, in a way, unfortunate that these words come to the reader by way of print. They do, to be sure, carry their message with grace and conviction. And reading this book is an exciting introduction to Wilma's thinking. But the printed word lacks the wonderful verve, excitement, and yes, even joy that her presence bestowed on them. She had a lovely voice, low-key but vibrant, with the added force of the beautiful and vital woman projecting it. She could enthrall an audience with her wit and humor. Her cool and impregnable logic could also infuriate (pp.136-137). You "caught" her message.

Wilma's ear was always cocked for a call to places where her voice was needed. And it was widely needed – as consultant, as inspiration, as cheer-leader. And the responses she elicited nourished and supported her. Such activism fulfilled her sense of a calling.

The Preface recounts how Wilma re-constructed her activism in the direction of written words and less face-to-face contacts with an audience. I think there was a real sacrifice here. Like Robert Frost's traveller at the fork in the road, she chose the, to her, harder road, feeling that she had many miles to go before she slept. She refers to "the self-discipline it required of [her] to focus on this work, however related, when needs and opportunities abound to impact on one's world and the [outer] world by other [more congenial] activities." (p.xii) She was giving up the excitement of the give-and-take of an audience. "Committing oneself to writing allows for no such luxuries of discussion and interpretation." (p.xi) There is urgency on every page. Further, in the past she had had the support of recognized status as an elected feminist leader, a state human rights commissioner, an academic professor. She was now writing with "no institutional organizational identity to nurture and affirm [her]." (p.xii)

I was caught up short when I read these words. I had not kept up with all her activities. I faulted myself as I re-viewed my contacts with Wilma. I had had the privilege of serving as dissertation mentor for her doctorate.[2] From time to time she had brought me pages of manuscript. I experienced these meetings as lively, excited, stimulating discussions between two women sharing her contribution to the Feminist Enlightenment. Only now does it occur to me that even she had needed nurturance, that she had needed protection from the "abundance of experience, ideas, and resource materials" that "nearly overwhelmed [her]", that she was literally being consumed by the urgency of her vision. She had seemed to have inexhaustible resources and to be always willing to expend them generously where needed. Had I let her down?

There proved to be no need for such concerns on my part. Actually committing herself to writing did not deprive her of affirming nurturance; she had never had to give up the opportunities to impact on the world. Her world would not permit it. She had remained in full stride to the end. Within the last few months of her life, she was a keynote speaker to women-in-sports, to women in leadership roles, to nurses; she was co-ordinator of a panel on feminism and peace for the 1985 U.N. Decade for Women Conference in Nairobi; she was helping others with their writing; and inspiring young activists to complete their dreams.

So here's to Wilma Scott Heide, a happy warrior armed with words and ideas, a lady with a lamp to illuminate a hitherto invisible female world, long may she live in the minds of appreciative readers of this book. She covered a great many miles before she slept.

– Jessie Bernard

1. I have, of course, taken liberties with Wordsworth's pronouns, substituting 'she' for 'he', 'her' for 'him', and 'one' for 'man', all changes in line with Wilma's own language preferences. (see p.119)

2. Wilma's dissertation was the starting point for this book. She added a few sections and updated some of the materials. Chapter 7 was not in the dissertation. She had reviewed and approved the edited manuscript. The editors Charlene Eldridge Wheeler and Peggy L. Chinn, "edited with the intent of enhancing the readability of the manuscript while maintaining Wilma's unique voice and writing style. Wilma wrote in an oral tradition, and we wanted to preserve this as much as possible." Two more books on Wilma are available, one by Eleanor Humes Haney *A Feminist Legacy: The Ethics of Wilma Scott Heide and Company* (1985), and one a collection of writings in tribute to Wilma edited by Eleanor Humes Haney (in progress). There will doubtless be other books on this visionary happy warrior.

PREFACE

I have completed these chapters of my reflections and prophecy with a mixed sense of exhilaration and of the need to be finite. My relative abundance of experience, ideas, and resource materials both nurtured and nearly overwhelmed me. Writing these chapters has been a growing, changing experience in several regards. I want to share the ways I had to change my patterns of the previous decade.

Writing is not new to me. Writing for reading only, as compared to much of my previous writing for speeches or other oral presentations that were secondarily published, required imagining of whose eyes and minds would be contacted by my thoughts. In a speech or presentation, one can know almost immediately if a theme, an idea, a concept, a phrase, a style or a philosophy is being communicated. One can ad lib, elaborate, modify, eliminate parts as feedback suggests. Committing oneself to writing allows for no such luxuries of discussion and interpretation.

Neither is a reader a captive as is an audience, who generally will remain out of politeness simply because her/his departure would be noticed. A solitary reader can simply lay aside a paper or silently close a book with no one the wiser, surely not the writer. Capturing, or rather engrossing, and retaining the reader is a constant motivation and challenge. The act of writing presumes something worth the effort of both writer and reader. It is presumptuous to write at all, let alone to publish for others to read.

For the previous decades, people have listened to and/or read me, partly because of who I was as an elected feminist leader, an appointed human rights commissioner, an institutionally affiliated behavioral scientist, professor or nurse. These past several years, I have had no institutional or organizational identity to nurture and affirm me. True, there are others whose support is vital. In truth, this makes a difference because the writing experience is largely for me, though it should ultimately benefit others as well.

Much of my work has important gratifications to and for me; because its potential for transforming the nation and the world are immediate and compelling. What I'm expressing is the self-discipline it required of me to focus on this work, however related, when needs and opportunities abound to impact on one's world and the world by other activities. That I may have succeeded at all in my focus is a tribute to the realization that the discipline, the reflective time, and some attention to writing skills should have some long-term benefits for whatever I am about.

For the reader, I have, hopefully, conveyed some sense of what feminism portends, combined scholarship with my visions, shared some breadth and depth of feminist potential, and tried to write with whatever clarity possible when prophecy is nearly denuded by the dailiness of the status quo. My advocacy of change is not the closet variety. Passion is closeted, in this case, at a peril to justice. Higher academia as well as others must recognize that justice requires a covenant with perceived truth that embraces passion and transcends any single discipline.

If my perceptions, reflections, scholarship, and projections indeed convey real and potential truths, feminism may indeed portend redefinitions of power. Reconceptualizing power itself can mean the empowerment of us all so that the power of love (in the sense of caring for ourselves and each other) can exceed the love of power to control others. This writing sought to help convey that humanity may be yearning for that covenant with truth for the life and health of us all.

CHAPTER ONE

QUEST FOR OUR HUMANITY VIA HIGHER EDUCATION

An Open Letter to My Colleagues in Higher Education

Dear Sisters and Brothers:

I write this letter as a political activist, an educator, and, on a more personal level, as a parent of two college-age daughters. Originally this was conceived as an open letter to my daughters who were considering what, if any, formal education to pursue beyond high school. I was prepared to counsel my daughters to help them explore their feelings about what they thought they wanted and needed from higher education, and advise them to find and demand these imperatives from educators and administrators. It seemed that being part of the female majority of students, the prognosis for their power to be educated was never better.

Then I realized that it is my contemporaries as educators whom I wanted to address. My daughters may intuit what they need and want from education but they've not yet experienced "higher" education. We are the ones who "know" extant higher education by participation as students, purveyors, critics, administrators, trustees, and/or staff. We are the ones, ideally, in partnership with our daughters and our sons, who must covenant an educational quality that transcends the orientations of affluent, straight white male values and content.

In the academic year 1974-1975, I spent some time as an invited guest-in-residence, without portfolio, at Wellesley College in Massachusetts. During the 1975 winter term, a young woman student there was physically raped on the Wellesley campus. Though relatively infrequent (about 10 reported cases in the past seven years), it was not the first such tragedy. Justifiable outrage was rampant. Urgent meetings were held, guidelines for behavior of women at Wellesley were drawn up, and an escort system was developed so women wouldn't be "out" alone. Personnel characterized the campus community as stunned. A suburban campus in an affluent community seems not to be many people's image of a setting for such a violation as rape. Money earlier budgeted, but not used, to upgrade campus security was quickly allocated. For the first time, the college administration even accepted and put into operation the idea to include women as part of the security personnel. The college sponsored a self-defense class, taught by a man, that has since been integrated into the ongoing physical education program.

The major preoccupations were with security and the behaviors of the women, implicitly suggesting that what the women did or did not do made the generative and significant difference. It would be accurate to state, that except for a few up-front feminists, the rape and rape in general at Wellesley was perceived as essentially a violent sexual assault, which it also was. It was not perceived as primarily a political act with forced sexual intercourse as part of its manifestation. The response was reactive – not proactive. Liva Baker, a Smith College alumna, writing about the Seven (now Six) Sister Colleges, including Wellesley notes:

> The real problem of the Seven Sisters is that singly and collectively they found themselves consistently faced with the same dilemmas women in the larger society faced, and they chose to solve [sic] them in the same way, demonstrating institutional timidity and humility and becoming severely limited within the obvious societal and academic parameters. Their survival depends on . . . whether they can become truly innovative, can begin to think in terms of lowering the water instead of routinely raising the bridge, in terms of curriculum, faculty, financing, administration: whether they have dreams in their

heads, and whether they can discover the means of making them come true. (in *I'm Radcliffe, Fly Me: The Seven Sisters and the Failure of Women's Education.* Macmillan, New York. 1976, p. 216.)

Wellesley College has *dreams which include careerism and serious education of women but that alone does not a feminist institution make. To the extent that academic institutions are not feminist, they are indeed sexist and androcentric. In order for women's colleges to be valid, they must become feminist. Failing to become feminist, they will continue to perpetuate the rape of women – intellectually, socially, politically, economically, psychologically and spiritually as well as physically. I would assert that co-educational institutions need, even more strongly, to confront the dilemmas of women and male chauvinists consequent to patriarchy, with feminist perspectives, values and commitments if educational validity is envisioned.*

Having noted the general political naïveté about physical rape as a serious symptom of deeper problems and the typical re-active behaviors, I may be optimistic to assume that educators will appreciate the more sophisticated phenomena of intellectual and other rape of women by and in the not yet feminist institution. To do that, I will define rape – in the generic sense – as a penetration and violation of the person, her body, her mind, her spirit. Rape is violence. Rape is the application of real or implied force and power. In the physical phenomenon of rape, the rapist compels the victim to submit to penile-vaginal sexual intercourse or other related assaults on the person against her will.

Just as a feminist consciousness is apparently necessary to understand physical rape as a symptomatic, sexually expressed but essentially political act of power of men against women, so may feminist analyses be necessary to recognize the intellectual rape of women in institutions that are patriarchal in style, values, curriculum. In educational rape – in the sense of penetration and violation of consciousness, of intellect, of thought processes – it is the near total control of knowledge by and for men that does violence to persons by diminishing women and glorifying men. I consider these issues not only matters of educational validity but of ethical integrity. I define integrity as a state of being whole, entire and undiminished. This meaning applies to individuals, areas of knowledge, and institutional practices.

We who are feminists know how to be dispassionate (as we are repeatedly exhorted to be), to pretend objectivity that is psuedo at best, distanced from reality at worst. But we eschew psuedo-objectivity. Instead, we opt for the honesty of accountability for our subjective involvement in and with our subjects. Things and automatons are objective; people are subjective entities. We are responsible for our actions, like our teaching and our ethics. It is not responsible to pretend that education and educators of all disciplines are value free, because it is not true.

A pro-active approach would long since have acknowledged the reality that most higher education courses and curricula are, in effect, men's studies, albeit by other names. This results in a profound social illiteracy about women's past, present, and future that amounts to miseducation. Indeed, the illiteracy is so fundamental and serious that I would recommend that any institution that has any degree requirements include women's studies as requirements for receipt of an educational degree. The same, of course, is true about studies of people of color.

I define education as a process of developing one's faculties to grow, through both formal and informal higher education. The educational, intellectual, and counseling needs of women simply have not and cannot be met without revised curricular and other programs that include the truth and the whole truth about women, our realities and potential, and indeed, the truth about men. The revisions will require substantial compensatory re-education of most faculty, counselors, and administrators. The quest for our humanity through higher education requires a profound re-orientation – to be humanely valid. There is today no university in the sense of universal truths; there are only semi-versities of essentially white, heterosexual androcentric thought patterns. The thoughts and experiences of authentic (ie, self-defined, self-authored) women of color, of homosexual people, are nearly absent. Whatever the conscious intent of patriarchal training (as compared to education, as I would define it), the consequent damages to women specifically and to society generally derive from, generate and perpetuate the fragile male ego and its accompanying stress; the stress to perform, to "prove" itself, to assuage its insecurities – all as a consequence of the male as the ostensible center of the universe.

Although many feminists have administered to and co-designed programs and generated changes that forever have or will transform society, still higher education has the audacity and myopia to actually question if such feminists and minorities can teach and administer. No, we are not technicians, we are not pedantic teachers; we are prophets and visionaries of a future that needn't pass academic understanding until years later. Our community, our neighborhoods, our world that we would make our home is our academy and can be yours. Pierce the veil of the commonplace and embrace us who are feminists and other change agents and you will embrace your alienated selves and transfuse the very life blood of academia to celebrate the fullness of life.

In art, in law, in philosophy, in science, in sociology and anthropology, in the humanities, in economics, in agriculture, in history, in academia and elsewhere, the ultimate dialectic may be combining the positive and informative dimensions of feminine and masculine, the subjective and objective, the emotional and rational, the micro and macro aspects of knowledge into the transcendent syntheses of feminism that leads to a balance of mind, of emotions, of soul. Now, that's a vital core of genuine affirmative action to change not only the cast of characters in academia, but also the scripts and the scripting of higher education. That is truly educational: a quest for our humanity.

This letter is lengthy, my colleagues, but the process of un becoming so traditionally academic as to be irrelevant to most of humanity and destructive to those who are not affluent white heterosexual males, requires extended covenanting of the feminist ethos in the human interest if we are to become educators. Our fidelity, our commitment is to truth.

With cheers and ultimate optimism

Wilma Scott Heide

Semi-versities: Intellectual Rape

Having begun with an open letter to my colleagues in academe, this chapter will explore the near total male control of what has been considered thought, knowledge, science, art, philosophy as a rape of our minds, especially women's. The fact that most higher education is essentially white male studies, albeit with other titles, produces and perpetuates a profound social illiteracy about the majority of people who are not male and/or not white. Corrective women's studies, feminist studies and studies of people of color may be considered affirmative action requirements in the quest for our humanity. In examining major areas of academic pursuits, I will acknowledge that no discipline or educator is value-neutral, and that education itself means change and is implicitly and explicitly political.

Sexism represents the historically first and basic form of human oppression; it has served to sanction the *idea* of oppression and the division of people into ruler and ruled, dominant and dominated. Racism, classism, ageism, homophobia are power dynamics that follow this paradigm and thus the sanctioning of the *phenomenon* of oppression. All forms of oppression are profoundly inhumane and incompatible with education as I define it. Feminism both challenges oppression and portends enormous potential in eliminating it. The issue is not one of relative seriousness or importance of different oppressions, but rather a matter of acknowledging the original model of dehumanization from which other manifestations and patterns derived.

Sexism has deep historical roots, and is perpetuated by the partial study of men's history. It is impossible to discover and integrate knowledge of the history of women without rediscovering and reconceptualizing the endeavor of history itself.[1] Most of what passes for history is ahistorical because it simply ignores, trivializes, or minimizes the past events of the majority of the population. So too, with science, with sociology, art and every other area of human knowledge; ostensible science is not valid if the truth about women is distorted, minimized and/or absent, and knowledge about men is distorted and exaggerated.

Existing Semi-versities

Essentially, women's colleges have been the only likely alternatives to male-dominated higher education, but few of those have been administered by women who articulate changed consciousness and commitments. Henry Durant, a key founder of Wellesley College, is said to have stated at its 1875 founding that the real meaning of higher education for women was "revolt." Most Wellesley College folks were uncomfortable at best with my mention of that a century later when I was a guest-in-residence. About the same time in 1975, writer Nora Ephron (Wellesley '62) referred to her Alma Mater thusly: "This college is about as meaningful to the educational process in America as a perfume factory is to the national ecomony."[2,p.36] Florynce Kennedy, a black feminist civil rights attorney and phrase-maker, referred to Wellesley College as a "cupcake institution" in a speech givenat Wellesley in the Spring of 1975. These are harsh assessments. But these assessments are accurate because Wellesley and most other women's colleges do exactly the job to which they are committed – maintaining male-defined education.

In essence, women's colleges provide for women:
- academic "education" as good (or bad?) as men's colleges;
- education that promotes essential adjustment to and participation in perpetuation of gender specific roles;
- little or no opportunity to participate as feminists outside or inside the college to challenge and change the status quo, with notable individual exceptions; and
- subtle or blatant subversion of any will of students, faculty, and administration to translate the ethics of conscience to "real world" political action.

The imposed paralysis of the will to change is the most serious indictment of most women's colleges. By implicitly and explicitly accepting and emulating patriarchal instituions and values, the capacity of students to develop and express a contrary will of their own is either a coincidental happening in spite of negative sanctions or the absence of positive sanctions, or that capacity is disempowered to render women virtually impotent.

It is important that these observations and assessments of most women's colleges not be interpreted as *blaming the victims* – women's colleges and the women therein. I have profound sympathy for the colleges and the women in them, yet must mourn their rape and disempowerment which could have been prevented if their implicitly feminist foundings had been translated to explicitly feminist ethics, aspiration, education and values. I want the power of the concept of rape to be understood to have intellectual and spiritual manifestations against the will of their victims.

Harvard Semi-versity represents a typical approach to the "problem" of women's education. Harvard is still considered by some folks to represent the zenith of educational excellence. In 1976, Harvard took as "his" wife, Radcliffe, the neighboring women's college. The marriage ocurred to provide economic security and convenience for Radcliffe.[3] The newly merged faculty of arts and sciences has about half a dozen courses out of 700 that deal explicitly with women's experiences, only one or two of these offer a feminist perspective.[4] The alleged "advantages" to women of semi-versity marriages are question-able. The men and women of such a patriarchal marriage become as one, and that one is the men or the male institution; otherwise it would now be called Harvard-Radcliffe or Radcliffe-Harvard.

The sheer power and prestige of the Harvard name, when examined and exposed by feminists, represents a devastating rape of women. It may be overly optimistic to hope that the Harvard Corporation of straight, affluent white males who run it are educable in the forseeable future. I am, indeed, suggesting a wake for Radcliffe College's convenient "marriage." Further-more, a moratorium on the mythology about Harvard's "excellence" would be in the national interest. It is precisely because Harvard is considered so excellent that it can perpetuate it's mis-education.

Feminist Transcendence

Prior to a decade or so ago, sex role stereotyping was not only normal, indeed it was considered "natural." While feminism is not yet considered normal, it is indeed very natural. In a healthy society, the natural is normal. Feminism, which transcends the gendering of knowledge, asks who *are* the educators when many of the most profound changes and movements originate outside academia. Knowledge is empowerment; who are the gatekeepers of knowledge? Indeed, should there be any gates that reinforce an unjust status quo? Should we replace gates with "guts" to covenant with the truth about humanity's quest for itself?

Feminism – as philosophy, as values transformation, as ethical re-orientation – critiques not only obviously "bad" scholarship but areas of supposed knowledge that lack women's thoughts and experiences, and thus the integrity of wholeness and entirety. Much of what is generally *considered* "good" scholarship, "good" sociology, "good" economics, "good" philosophy or psychology, "good" political or other science, "good" theology, "good" history, is simply invalid on feminist terms, partly because it is androcentric and partly because it ignores or devalues both women and "feminine" values.

Feminism eschews the narrowness and arbitrariness of departmentalizing and specializing, of knowing more and more about less and less. Feminism critiques the disciplines themselves and transcends compartmentalizing of knowledge by transdisciplinary processes that degender knowledge itself. Feminism is a process of becoming and being; it includes *un*-becoming what sex stereotyping has previously taught us as appropriate for women only or for men only. Feminism validates the wisdom of our senses and our experiences.

Most important, feminism generates and nurtures precious visions of possibilities for our humanity. Feminism is also a powerful philosophy, ideas and visions, indeed, gestalts of creative leaps to new possibilities. It is ironic that feminism is not yet considered "legitimate" by some folks in and out of academia. That's one of the risks of exploring unfamiliar ideas and leaving the protective custody of familiar processes to envision and create the yet untried. I would posit that the genesis of alleged "illegitimacy" may well derive from the patriarchal and androcentric characteristics of traditional education, culture, society and its institutional ethos and styles which feminism confronts and makes illegitimate.

Acts of Commission and Omission

The traditional intellectual and spiritual penetration of human consciousness represents a rape that is against women's will as much as any physical rape; it occurs by acts of omission and/or commission. Not only is much traditional scholarship against women's will, it is little informed by the will of women, especially by the will of women and men who reject the tenets and manifestations of patriarchy. The overt commissions of sex discrimination in academia, as evidenced in employment and admission practices, are serious violations of women that are well documented. These overt violations are technically accessible to the remedies of civil rights laws and executive orders. It is the covert but institutionalized practices of academia that I want to address – practices that are often denied to result in oppression of women and which are not yet accessible by legal remedies.

Language

The conceptual and linguistic use of male imagery and language as the alleged generic for all people and the presumed norm for all humans is still a central rape of all women by exclusion of women from consciousness. This practice in academia or anywhere else distorts conceptualization of what has been, what is, and what will be included in and about human affairs. Examples are courses, curricular materials, and also discussions that refer variously to: *man* and *his* world; *mankind; man* and *his* philosophies, *his* ideas, *his* problems, *his* achievements, *his* government, *his* art, *his* literature, *his* theology, *his* politics, *his* family, *his* children, *his* socialization, *his* civilization, *his* public affairs, *his* media, *his* cities, *his* farms, *his* works, *his* wars (and *that's* pretty accurate), ad nauseum and ad alienation of women and girls on some level of consciousness. The words 'he' and 'him' have woman-denial effects; these words place females in the category of subsumed, other, not normal, or simply missing from imagery and consciousness.

Again and again and again, some academic people deny the effects on consciousness of single sex (male) referents, issue disclaimers in writing and speech by suggesting 'man' and 'he' includes 'woman' and 'she', or try to trivialize the issues by implying these are "feminist hang-ups." Any reader who still doubts the effects on consciousness of single sex referents is advised to substitute 'woman' and 'her', and 'she' instead of 'he' whenever the referent is supposed to be both male and female, or is unspecified. Do this in *all* writing and speech for one year. I've suggested this experiment in speeches, meetings, and writings since 1970 and requested feedback on the experiences of people with the courage and sense of adventure to seriously try to use the reversal. To date no one who has tried it and reported back to me *ever* again will suggest that the issue of sexism in the language is a trivial, irrelevant, and/or unimportant determinant of consciousness about human beings and our affairs. 'Woman' does include 'man', 'she' does include 'he', unlike the reverse. Personification via language is a powerful method to evoke and include images – or exclude them. Male-only language is an intolerable practice for any academic setting that pretends to a valid quest for our humanity.

Male-only language extends far beyond the obvious gender specific nouns and pronouns. A feminist approach to language is based on valuing the "feminine" principles in language.

Words produce images that are often associated with sex polarization and the sexual caste system (a la "femininity" for women and "masculinity" for men) and are apparently basic to the essentially male-defined existence and being. Ontology, the ostensible "science of being," has been androcentric, thus contaminating our transcendent gynandry and limiting our vision of humanity's possibilities. As feminists perform cultural interpretation of many of women's and men's experiences of "feminine" and "masculine," ontology and other areas of knowledge may become more scientific (meaning true) because of becoming more wholly human.

The Table on page 13 lists apparent feminine/masculine, female/male, woman/man bifurcations and dichotomies evident in academia, in its imagery, in values, in behaviors and in society. The words in the Table suggest concepts, images, values, behaviors, traits and other phenomena. In the left-hand column are those phenomena often associated with the right hemisphere of the brain – with the feminine, with females, with women. In the right-hand column are those phenomena often associated with the left hemisphere of the brain – with the masculine, with males, with men.[5] In the gendering of knowledge and its pursuit, "masculine" is valued. "Feminine" is devalued or so it seems, and the "higher" the educational "level," the more this is made to appear true and valid (sic). In the middle column are phenomena that I call "feminist transcendent" – a combination of positive dimensions of "feminine" and "masculine" phenomena into a more advanced phenomenon.

I call the transcendent concepts feminist because the transcendence is corrective of the prevailing devaluing and privatizing of the "feminine," as well as of women. Women are erroneously considered the sole possessors and practitioners of "feminine" potential.[6] Men are often erroneously considered the sole possessors and practitioners of "masculine" potential.[7] Concepts based on the "masculine" principle are:

- often more valued than the "feminine;"
- often given more credence particularly in public affairs and behaviors (especially, but not only, for men);
- more dominant and dominating than "feminine" phenomena;
- causative of the split, dichomoties and bifurcations themselves because men learn to deny or privatize their "feminine" dimensions.

Maleness, a biological part of one's identity, is often and erroneously equated with "masculine" which refers to socially learned phenomena. Likewise, femaleness, a biological part of one's identity, is often and erroneously equated with "feminine" which also refers to socially learned phenomena. Therefore, in identifying "feminine" and "masculine" concepts I exclude the sex-specific reproductive anatomy and potential from the repertoires and descriptions often designated erroneously as "masculine" and "feminine." Both "feminine" and "masculine" behaviors, interests, traits, values, concepts are *naturally* the repertoires of both sexes.

Neither sex and no phenomenon is seldom (if ever) all "feminine" or all "masculine." Either "feminine" or "masculine" designed phenomena may situationally represent such intrinsic excellence that it may be transcendent. I've marked those items particularly promising of transdencence with a T. Where both "feminine" and "masculine" qualities seem transcendent and/or only a combination seems transcendent, I've designated the central column as "combination." I trust the reader will find the transcendent word images that escaped me at this writing or not worry. My hypotheses are part of an emerging process of thinking that pretends to no empirical documentation on my part.

Women's Studies

In the spring of 1975, a former Wellesley College faculty member told me, confidentially, that just two years previously she had been denied tenure at that college because she wanted to focus on women's studies. The reason given was that such an interest was not considered "serious scholarship." She is a highly competent scholar in her field who apparently can pursue her legitimate interests only where some feminist consciousness exists or she must use euphemistic subject titles. This is tantamount to a Black college denying the need or validity of Black Studies or a dental faculty not pursuing the study of teeth. Wellesley College is not alone among women's or coed colleges in its re-active and often reactionary and token response to women's studies courses.

The relatively recent proliferation of women's studies courses has occurred in spite of unfounded allegations of their being "unscholarly," "unprofessional," "lesbian," or "unnecessary." The courses are usually underfunded, sometimes uncredited, and academically undervalued. Women's studies are just beginning to be appreciated as corrective and affirmative action, yet such action is essential to cease the intellectual and spiritual rape of women – against the will of our authentic new consciousness – by acts of omission and commission. Indeed,

Feminist Transcendent Language

"FEMININE"	Transcendent FEMINIST/GYNANDROUS	"MASCULINE"
affective	discerning	cognitive
microcosm	universal	macrocosm
sharing	experiential	didactic
internal	sensual	external
re-active	pro-active	active
dependent	interdependent	independent
support	develop	control
intrinsic	integral	extrinsic
generative (T)	wholistic	linear
subordinate	coordinate	superordinate
implicit	*combination*	explicit
powerless	empowered	powerful
perceptual	*combination*	conceptual
body	self/human	mind
personal	personal is political and vice versa	political
passive†	creative	active
expressive	*combination*	instrumental
qualitative	*combination*	quantitative
intuitive	knowing	rational
cooperative (T)	comtestive††	competitive
compassionate	empathetic	dispassionate
private	integrated	public
process	process is product	product
serve	guide/contribute	lead
art	life	technologies
care	caring cure/ curative care	cure
humanities	knowledge	science
discuss	communicate	debate
organic	human	synthetic
emotional	existential	intellectual
soft (data)	experiential data	hard (data)
involved	friendly	distanced
personal	interpersonal	impersonal
wish	aspire	covet
student	co-learners	teacher
gynocentric	gynandrous	androcentric
comprehend	understand	master
subjective	relative	objective
nurturance	ad-ministration†††	management
feeling	being	thinking

(T) possible transcendent term
  † actually may be receptive
   †† word I created meaning "to test with others"
††† meaning "to minister to being"

some folks at some institutions are beginning to value women's studies via feminist scholarship as a desirable model of wholistic education about the artificial academic turfs and limitations of departmentalizing of androcentric academia. Sangamon State, Illinois' Public Affairs institution where I spent a few years recently, is one such example where this is beginning to happen.

The direct relationship between the fundamental oppression of sexism and the related oppression of racism is exemplified in higher education. Michelle Russell writes in *Quest* "An Open Letter to the Academy" (meaning higher education) that is deeply moving, provocative and relevant.[8] The letter might come from Black women, from Chicana, from Hispanic, from Puerto Rican, from Native American, from Asian American women and indeed from men of color, and surely, from those of any race who are economically impoverished. She addresses her remarks to white women in the Academy, knowing the white men may need them even more. She acknowledges the interdisciplinary possibilities and institutional restructuring potential of women's studies. Ms. Russell writes:

> I would like to widen the discussion to address the responsibility of women's studies to those outside the academy's walls; the mass of women whose lives will be fundamentally affected by the version of reality developed there, but who, as yet, have no way of directly influencing your direction.[8,p.70]

She characterizes the Academy as an ivory tower with an intellectual predisposition "to regard anything dead as good and the living as suspect and intrusive."[8,p.72] In Ms. Russell's view the academy is a sanctuary which lies in suspension somewhere between the 15th and 19th centuries, with colonization more prevalent than civilization, and barbarism triumphing in the guise of progress.[9] She writes:

> And the primary political and cultural role of Western women and the academy has been to rationalize it [racism] . . . as a victimized, accomplice population in this process . . . Your oppression and exploitation have been more cleverly masked than ours, more delicately elaborated. The techniques, refined. You were rewarded in minor ways for docile and active complicity in our dehumanization.[8,p.75]

Ms. Russell asks the academy and women's studies what and whose stories we will tell?

> The question is this: How will you refuse to let the academy separate the dead from the living, and then, yourselves declare allegiance to life? As teachers, scholars and students, how available will you make your knowledge to others as tools of their own liberation?[8,p.77]

Ms. Russell writes knowingly of those forced outside academia, or who were never in, and for whom pedagogy has become peripatetic. Feminist scholars must create our own teaching opportunities if we are to create change. Change agents are not welcome as ongoing residents in academia – the processes in which we're engaged don't fit "neatly into 50 minute hours or a disciplinary definition of field of study."[8,p.79] We're variously called: "scholar in residence," "visiting lecturer" or "professor," "guest" or "consultant." The titles are actually academic euphemisms for the accurate feminist-at-large, change agent or revolutionary.

> ...we carry our texts in our heads and on our backs ...our wit must stick and have the veracity of experience digested, not just books well remembered. We teach in the world...When hard questions are put to us, we cannot say with smugness, "That is not my field;" we can only say, "I don't know."[8,p.79]

The feminist challenge is to find answers and share them in and out of academia.

The arts provide an example of the potential of women's studies in higher education. Art scholars have taken a fundamental corrective action by discovering our foremothers and sisters who were and are great artists. The evaluation of "great" is surely, in part, subjective. The life experience of living as a woman must be expressed and critiqued by women, for a change. From my perspective, art is great if it:

- connects life and living with the living;
- communicates our thoughts, our feelings, our impressions, our passions, our visions;
- both captures the dailiness of life and liberates our spirits to soar beyond the mundane;
- expresses both simplicity and complexity.

Women's studies and feminist artists are documenting and removing the enormous barriers to women's artistry as painters, sculptors, dancers, composers, handicrafters, craftswomen, musicians and humorists.[10] In fact, many of the qualities required of artists such as sensitivity, awareness of nuances of colors and of behaviors, grace, subjectivity, expressiveness, appreciation of beauty and form have been especially expected of women, and indeed considered by some the special talents of women. There is no generic difference in women's art and men's art, except as differential life experiences influence it.

Still, those who oppose feminism, academicians who would derogate women's studies, encourage women to be art historians and not artists. The question "Why have there been no great women artists?" is false. There have been and are great women artists, in spite of enormous institutionalized barriers.

> The fault lies not in our stars, our hormones, our menstrual cycles, or our empty internal spaces but in our institutions and our "education" – education understood to include everything that happens to us from the moment we enter, usually head first, into this world . . . The miracle is, in fact, that given the overwhelming odds against women, so many of us have managed to achieve so much excellence.[11,p.67]

Gendering of Knowledge

"Masculine/feminine" dualities are alive in academia. There are both individual and universal consequences of assiduously and unnaturally training girls and women for "femininity" only, and boys and men for "masculinity" only. The very existence of super-imposed training demonstrates it is *not* natural.

I urge the reader to think about the individual and universal consequences of assiduously and unnaturally training girls and women for "femininity" only and boys and men for "masculinity" only. Then think about the related gendering of knowledge as we examine some of the extant academic disciplines and departments. The dangerous consequences of the masculine/feminine dualities are graphically conveyed in the Foreword to the Roszak's book *Masculine/Feminine*. "Feminine" and "masculine" postures are depicted as a devastating game that women and men are playing, with each one's behavior reinforced by the behavior of the other. As "he" and "she" become increasingly caught up in the game, they must each deny parts of themselves, to their own discomfort and with the price of growing contempt of the other. For him the reward for playing the masculinity game is power; for her it is the security his power confers on her. While she is "stiffling under the triviality of her femininity," the world is "groaning under the terrors of his masculinity." The Roszak's pose the question: "How do we call off the game? [12,p. viii]

Feminists have called off the masculine-feminine game in direct and subtle ways. We are doing it in research,[13] in writing, in assertiveness training for women, in non-sexist childrearing,[14] in sociology and politics of feeling and touch,[15] in feminist theology,[5] in futurist alternatives,[16] in women's studies curricula,[17] and organization.[18] Feminist and other change agents are using national, local organizations and groups, conferences, new lifestyles, legislation, changed public policy to prevent the world from not only groaning, but being literally destroyed by the terrors of masculinity. A vital part of the imperative is transcending the *either/or* – "feminine" for women only, "masculine" for men only – values and concepts. The gendering of knowledge is perpetuated by the dominance in academia of "masculine" orientations and practices and males and the devaluing of "feminine" realities and potential as well as women ourselves.

Misogyny, the hatred of women, is a powerful tool used in academia to perpetuate the gendering of knowledge. Indeed, "misogyny should itself become a central subject of inquiry, rather than continue as a desperate clinging to old, destructive fears and privileges."[16,p.27] It is the misogyny, *not* its study, that is indecent and unfit whether in academia or elsewhere. How ironic that the business of "civilization" (sic – colonization), such as it is, has been allegedly accomplished mostly by men, though it is mostly women who have had the literal civilizing effect; traditional sources are profound distortions of human history. Adrienne Rich addresses the importance of examining this irony:

> How this came to be, and the process that kept it so, may well be the most important question for the self-understanding and survival of the human species; but the extent to which civilization [sic] has been built on the bodies and services of women – unacknowledged, unpaid, and unprotected in the main – is a subject apparently unfit for scholarly decency.[18,p.25]

The destructive reality of total, or even near total, male control of human thought, systems of knowledge, belief systems, educational institutions and processes, is a part of the terror under which the world is groaning. Most men, even those who are personally decent and aspire to be humane, use male-only language, exclude from or tokenize women in their projects, ignore the feminist connections and implications and even the existence of the women's movement, exhibit androcentric values and hierarchies and erase women's experience. The work of Harvard's Lawrence Kohlberg is an example of how women's experience is erased in creating theoretical "truths." His research on moral development has used a single configuration (linear limitations) of male-only responses as the basis for an allegedly universal theory of moral development. His theory leaves women at stage three of his six stage moral development levels, ie, women as moral inferiors to men.[19]

All existing academic disciplines and departments provide overwhelming evidence of the gendering of knowledge. In the following sections are a few examples where feminist vision could provide the healing shift toward de-gendering of knowledge.

Sociology

In sociology, there is currently no theory of feelings and of emotions. Partly this is from the discipline's attempts to be recognized as a real science, androcentrically defined as objective and quantifiable, cognitive, intellectual, conscious and rational. Disclaimed or devalued are the emotional, the sentimental, the unconscious, the affective feelings that influence social phenomena. Significantly, in some instances the terms 'emotional' and 'sentimental' have come to connote excessive or degenerate forms of feeling. Feeling, sentiment and emotion have been associated with the "feminine," with women, though these are characteristics of all humans. Emotion, of course, is necessary for and derives from that which moves, which serves as catalyst or stimulant to action. Much of sociology emphasizes the conscious, cognitive, instrumental, rational actors,[20] and devalues the unconscious, emotional, expressive, affective actor. A feminist and a gynandrous sociology might convey the transcending sentient[15] actors who are both affective and cognitive and thus present a more accurate, fully human knowledge of people as we really are.

Sociology that merely intellectualizes is inadequate to understanding interrelations of people, groups, institutions, and societies. Sociology's real function has been to provide jobs for mostly white males to interpret and strengthen patriarchal world views. Interestingly and not surprisingly, sociology did not foresee the revolt of minorities of color in the United States, nor of the poor and of women. Predictability is ostensibly one reason given for sociology and other disciplines.

Philosophy

Philosophy is defined in the *American College Dictionary* as: "1. the study or science of the truths or principles underlying all knowledge or being (or reality)."[21,p.910] Sometimes a favorite philosophy or philosopher is referred to as respectively, "seminal thinking" or as a "seminal thinker." 'Seminal' is defined variously as first principles or fundamental principles and as having possibilities of future development. The *American College Dictionary* defines 'seminal' as "of, pertaining to, or of the nature of semen." 'Semen' is of course, defined as "male seed or sperm."[21,p.1100-1101] *Precisely!* 'Seminal' is a misnomer when intended to mean first, fundamental and/or universal principles because 'seminal' is male *only* and thus a part, not the whole of humankind. Philosophy – itself alleging universality – and the philosophies of fields of knowledge have been either all male at worst or androcentric at best, and thus not universal on their own terms.

Carol Gould writes that traditional and much contemporary "philosophy," especially "essentialist philosophy," emphasizes *abstract* universality.[22] At the same time, philosophy denies the *concrete universality of women,* or subordinates women to men, or makes women an accidental and thus disqualified part of the alleged universal norm – which includes males only. The traits, behaviors, kinds of experiences expected of males only are defined as the rational, the essentially human, the norm, the universal. Alleged "female" behaviors *have been* a priori defined as irrational and *currently* are implied to be nonrational. Women are simply omitted or devalued.

Because male "essentialist" philosophy excludes and/or devalues over half the human family, it is not total and thus not essentialist, nor is it universal (I would call it semi-versal, if that). Much "philosophy" is a misnomer for what passes as philosophy because it purports that male is generic for human. Because a genuine philosophy that underlies all areas of knowledge and develops from feminist perspectives can open visions of new human possibilities, I trust the reader's heuristic pursuit of at least the philosophy of her/his area of knowledge, if not, indeed a critical study of traditional philosophy itself.

Science

As philosophy is biased and distorted so also is science. Science evolved partly due to dissatisfaction with the older philosophical approach to knowledge without empirical evidence for alleged first principles and universal truths. The *New Columbia Encyclopedia* defines science as: "...the organized body of knowledge concerning the physical world, both animate and inanimate, but a proper definition would have to include the attitudes and methods through which this body of knowledge is formed."[23,p.2850-2851] Who forms this knowledge? Who decides, develops and tests the hypotheses? Whose and what experiences determine the experiential foundations of what is concluded to be scientific validity? Scientists pride themselves on presumed rational impartiality. As with philosophy and philosophers, what is termed "rational" generally turns out to have androcentric formulations and mostly male formulators, which invalidates impartiality of concept and/or method on its own terms of universality.

Historians of science seem willing to analyze every other social variable for its impact on the organization of knowledge, except the variable of sex. The scientific method itself thus sanctifies itself into what Mary Daly calls "methodolatry," which creates a tyranny that limits insights about what was and is, inhibiting new discoveries.[24] Science has become something of a new religion which claims objective neutrality, though it remains patriarchal. Objective neutrality is a demonstratable impossibility because patriarchy is male-dominated and thus biased and not neutral. It is precisely the ostensibly scientific method – and the would-be scientist's conscious rejection and ignorance of the subjective and a-rational in human activity,[25] allegedly women's domain – that emphatically invalidates so much of science on its own terms in claims to truth and knowledge. Patriarchal science is esoterically limited, not profound, and not wholistic.

A male would-be humanist, Everett Mendelsohn, sounds promising at first glance: "A reconstructed science would value truth but also compassion. It would have an inbuilt ethic that would defend[26] both being and living, that is, knowledge that would be non-violent, non-coersive, non-exploitive, non-manipulative..."[25,p.52] Mendelsohn fails to recognize the fact that labels of "pseudoscience" are placed on feminist attempts to humanize science; he does not mention the violent drive underground of the healing science and midwifery of wisewomen. He fails to note the positive correlations between science's masculinization and its defeminization, its elitism, apparent indifference to values, and methological rigidity. He does advocate science for human needs and science for the public good, but appears unknowing or unaware that feminist value transformations and ethical covenants are necessary steps to achieve science for the people.

Contrast Mendelsohn's view to that of scientist and feminist Rita Arditti:

> In the scientific environment a style and organization evolved from Bacon's ideas: Nature was to be conquered and scientists organized themselves in a quasi-military fashion to assault *her.* [emphasis added, and note, nature, ships, hurricanes and other phenomena to be controlled are always "she" and "her"] ... The sexual dynamics (of science workplaces) are such that few women manage to develop the skills and the self-confidence necessary to survive in an extremely competitive environment...Out of our experience of support groups in the women's movement, some of us have learned that conditions which enable people to work creatively and joyfully are practically nonexistent in the scientific milieu.
>
> We have to question the process by which scientific work is accomplished and its product. [And, I would add, the process *is* part of the product]. We are taught to approach problems with a purely cerebral attitude and *not* to bother with the consequences or ramifications of our work. The pressure is 'to keep things separate': scientific inquiry on one hand and human concerns on the other. This way of working leaves little room for our development as human beings and opens the door to the creation of exploitative technologies. We stand powerless, producing knowledge that can be used against people in a variety of ways. The myth of value-free science is being replaced by an awareness that science perpetuates and generates values...
>
> The task that seems of primary importance, for both women and men, is to convert science from what it is today, a social institution with a conservative function and the defensive stand, into a liberating and healthy activity; science with a soul which would respect and love its objects of study and stress harmony and communication with the rest of the

universe. When science fulfills its potential and becomes a tool for human liberation we will not have to worry about women 'fitting in,' because we will probably be at the forefront of that 'new' science.[27,p.26]

As a biologist doing research at Harvard for six years and now a leader in experimental and experiential higher education in the United States, Dr. Arditti knows whereof she speaks. Her article traces how Aristotle believed women inferior to men in all aspects; he "explained procreation as mainly the creative action of the male seed. This had great influence on latter-day biologists and 'scientists' and to this very day his hierarchical and dualistic thinking plagues many minds."[27,p.24]

The impact of feminism may yet be greatest in theoretical science which has been so inhospitable to women and so apparently ignorant of the subjective and a-rational in human activity (alias the "feminine" qualities). In the name of knowing more and more (sometimes less and less), knowledge is fragmented so that wholistic thought is actually weakened. The departments and disciplines of specialists quantify and instrumentalize the technical tangibles (masculine), while the real but intangible qualitative dimensions (feminine) become apparently unscientific and unimportant because they are immeasurable. Feminism is not anti-science; it is our demand for the whole truth and all possible knowledge that makes feminists the pre-cursors of genuine science.

Genetics

Genetics is defined as "the scientific-study of heredity."[23,p.1058] It is one more area of ostensible science where the "arrogance of male power"[28] is shatteringly discerned, as is the near imagelessness of women of all races, of minority men, and the poor. Whatever the intent, the consequences are politically potent. Genetics does not exist in a political or in an ethical vacuum. Genetics, concerned with the quality of life and, potentially who shall live, is not value-free. The cast of characters, the scripts, the givens of genetics determine who frames the issues, who determines what research, its uses and abuses, who allocates the public (and also private) funds to whom, and the consequences of genetic engineering and counseling.

Is it any wonder that some of us worry about cloning, about synthetic gene construction, about the ability not only to know (pre-birth) but to determine (pre-condition) the sex of the new organism?

Technology available has a way in human affairs of becoming technology applied. At the present stage of the (im)maturity of our society and culture, the facts are that males are preferred to females by most adults and most children. Until we mature enough to move from an androcentric to a gynandrous culture and society, the preference for males and maleness will persist for the simple reasons that there *are* legal, political, educational, religious, economic and other advantages to being male rather than female. Maleness itself, is neither intrinsically superior nor inferior to femaleness per se.[29,p.5]

Still, overt and covert female genocide policies and practices are neither without precedent nor potential – with human incubation outside the human maternal womb technologically possible, with female genocide an historical and indeed present reality in direct and indirect ways in some parts of the world. Women in the United States and world wide are becoming more "uppity," demanding of redefined and shared power. The majority of men in power, however, are threatened by feminism and often preoccupied with control and destruction of dissent. The consciousness of geneticists, their ethical bases and formulations, and their technological resources are not without influence in human affairs. One would have to be naive to completely eschew wariness.[30]

Sociobiology

Misogyny is not natural, however normal: it is learned. Tragically, misogyny is sometimes carefully taught, even unintentionally, in "higher education" by such disciplines or co-disciplines as sociobiology.

Sociobiology is a study of alleged biological bases of human social behavior. The discipline builds justification for biological determinism of social roles, especially when movements for change by underclasses portend some effectiveness. The race-IQ debate during the 60's civil rights movement in the United States is an example. Minority (in the USA) people's somewhat changing (improved) opportunities resulted in important social role changes. In the race-IQ debate, alleged superiority and inferiority of native, ie, "innate" intelligence based on race were promulgated – and persist to this day. "Race" itself is a biological fallacy: there are no "pure" races. Thus, the biological basis of behavior itself is without any means of genuine scientific support.

In the sociobiological studies of sex differences, the "equal-but-different" hypotheses do not supply differential evaluation. Women reportedly excel at skills allegedly requiring minimal mediation by higher cognitive processes. Cognitive processes are more highly valued than affective processes; the actual skills women have been allowed and expected to develop are the ones least valued by society.[31]

Sociobiological studies of sex differences have burgeoned since the regeneration of feminism in the 1960's, although such research is not new. Whatever differences have been noted generally (not universally) to exist are taken as "the givens" and the researchers set out to find biological bases for them. The research on sex differences is biased because the social behavior under study is learned in societies already premised on sex differential socialization.

Allegedly, biology is science and science is, reputedly, value-neutral and objective. The best research on sex differences is that of Macoby and Jacklin[32] who describe themselves as "feminist." These researchers accept the belief that biology has greater power and greater validity than sociology or psychology. Macoby and Jacklin conclude that the only reliably observed differences are female superiority in *all* language skills and male superiority in mathematical and spatial skills. These reported differences are not established until puberty, which makes explanations in terms of genetics and biology difficult at best. The paucity of support for sex differences, the lateness in their emergence, the known existence of great similarities, the discovery that some reported differences are actually extrapolations from (other) animal studies (always dangerous), and the reality that even tasks described as spatial are sometimes carried out by verbal processes and vice versa; all these and more unrefuted criticisms suggest limited validity and reliability in the best of studies.

If so few differences exist, why study and discuss them so extensively? Why take learned differences as givens implied in titles of articles and books, and thus reinforce by usage the idea of differences? The most validated of research actually demonstrates more similarities between people of each sex. Macoby and Jacklin's book, *Psychology of Sex Differences*, could more accurately have been titled *Psychology of Sex Similarities*, and probably even more so if they had premised their research on that hypothesis.[33]

Biological sex differences do exist. However, the androcentric science assumption that there is a dichotomy between biological and environmental influences on behavior is false. It is not enough to state that nurture (environment) acts on nature (biology) because that incorrectly assumes that nature is otherwise fixed. From the moment of conception, nature (biology) and nurture (environment) *interact* with each other so that their relative contributions become virtually inseparable. Statements about the singular biological origins of sexually dimorphic behavior that is social (as compared to biological or reproductive) are simply invalid.

Human behavior cannot be completely separated from biology. Neither can human behavior be causatively demonstrated to be generated by biology. Only when biology, sociology, psychology, anthropology and every other area of knowledge are liberated from the biases of *either/or* can any area be considered value-free and neutral. Sociobiology and the premise of biological determinism is not only bad science because it is *un* scientific – it is politically reactionary to feminism's intent to eliminate sexism.[34]

Agribusiness

Higher education addresses not only philosophy, art, sociology and science but also teaches about applied sciences and technology. Applied sciences allegedly generate knowledge that is useful in solving practical human problems. The areas of food, nutrition, agriculture and agri-business are important applied sciences in the context of world malnutrition, hunger and starvation, especially in what are euphemistically called developing countries and Third World countries (some of whose residents insist theirs is the First World).

> Women are responsible for 40-80% of all agricultural production in the developing countries . . . Men are being hired into the city and cash-producing work leaving women behind to work the land, tend the livestock, rear the children . . . The conclusion can be only too clear. If agricultural production and productivity are to increase, and thus help solve the problems of malnutrition and starvation, development planning must give an equal place to women, particularly rural women . . .[35]

That is the Agency for International Development (AID) Administrator John Gilligan speaking. However, AID's own record relative to women is poor. Less than 1% of its budget (.05 of 1%) goes to its one-year-old office for women in development, only 7.5% of its professional positions are held by women and those are at the lowest levels. Only recently is AID responding to women, and that due to some education by feminists. (I know this because I've been one of the educators.) There is an undeniable connection between social status and starvation, hunger, and malnutrition. Women who grow most of the world's food, prepare most of its meals, feed most of its children, are most likely to sicken and die from malnutrition.[36]

Most people in program and administration at AID must have at least a baccalaureate degree. Most people who write the books and design the programs on hunger, malnutrition, starvation and agriculture tokenly mention – or leave out completely -- women's vital roles and functions as farmers, as food producers, cultivators, planners and processors. AID, which employs and consults with personnel from higher education, continues to export patriarchy in countries where women have *had* some economic power as food producers; women are actually losing ground consequent to "development" programs.

Specifically, look at the World Agricultural Research Project, initiated by Harvard's prestigious School of Public Health and funded by the Ford Foundation for several years duration. This multi-disciplinary project was designed to find out why, with all the production progress of the past three decades, malnutrition and hunger have increased.[37] The introduction to the Project acknowledged the complex problems of research and capitalist agriculture production. The four general hypotheses reflect the awareness of:

- The profitability of agricultural production; regardless of nutritional and other needs of the people.
- The conduct of agricultural research in poor nations as alternatives to popular unrest.
- The limitations placed by the scientific/cultural milieau on agricultural research.
- That research, applied as new technology, increases the concentration of the wealthy and causes a decline in the welfare of the majority.[37]

The challenge of whether capitalism is in the human interest of the majority sounds laudable and promising, at least implicitly. However, although four of the nine professional project staff were women; nowhere is there mention of the roles of women, the potential of women, the majority of food and subsistence farmers, the enormous work loads of women as farmers, food processors, water carriers, homemakers, child caretakers and feeders. Questions about who owns the land, who raises the crops, who gets the technological aid and tools are missing. Feminists would not allow to go unnoticed and unaddressed the significance of sexism (by omission and commission) in creating and perpetuating hunger, malnutrition, and starvation. Once again, Harvard's low level of consciousness is part of the problem that augurs poorly for this project and its consequences in people's lives – and deaths.

Far removed from developing countries, down on the farm and in the publicly funded land-grant universities and community colleges, United States agribusiness and the related research thrives on patriarchy. Sociologist Sally Hacker carefully informs us how this is perpetuated:

> Agribusiness, like any hierarchical system is based on this rigid gendering of knowledge and experience that tells young men (women are made to feel unwelcome by statements like 'women might be in the way') which occupations, attitudes and behaviors to respect and which to ridicule and avoid. This applies even to specific classes. Students of horticulture ('feminine'?) are referred to as 'flower sellers.' Students were encouraged to think 'masculine,' think aggressive and think business (more than farming) management.[38,p.40]

Dr. Hacker asked about the role of the women in agribusiness and an instructor (male) replied: "The gals on the line? They are not considered a part of agribusiness. They do no decision-making at all."[38,p.42] Women and immigrant workers of mostly minority groups are exploited; the occupations are sex-segregated and with sex differential pay; infant and maternal mortality rates are more than 100% higher than the national averages, yet the victims are blamed for the problems caused by the white male club of agribusiness.[38]

Agribusiness and the training to prepare for it is supported and/or subsidized by public money. Is it uneducational to expect that those who train students, have the capacity and commitment to conceptualize, practice and teach justice? Of course, that's "political." And what of injustice? Is that not political?

Education in the Best Human Interest

Some may believe that educators cannot and should not be political; that we should distance ourselves from change ideologies, political movements and political action in the name of neutrality, objectivity and rationality. The fact is that education *is* political. 'Education' derives from the Latin words "educo," "educare" which means "to lead forth." That surely implies change from what is to something else – either in learning existing knowledge (real or alleged), or creation of new knowledge. There is no point to education without the anticipation of change. Education itself means empowerment.

Most higher education today is intended to produce the kind of change that fits one and adjusts one to the existing social, economic and political order.[39] Colleges teach old ideas not new ideas, and serve to reinforce the status quo differences based on one's sex, race, sexuality, and income: which in effect, give legitimacy to the affluent heterosexist white male club – a presumed ideal.[40]

Teaching and idealizing the anti-human phenomena of sexism, racism, classism, homophobia, and ageism is incompatible with education; and it is a political act of ommission or commission. We do not have the choice of whether or not to embrace the political. The choice largely involves which politics we choose.

To pretend an impossible neutrality and ostensibly not to choose is itself a political choice that is misleading. A claim of neutrality is dishonest at best. It either ignores the conflicts and confrontations of issues from which growth and change can occur, or accepts the traditional descriptions and definitions of others for fear of seeming political. In human affairs, to be apolitical is to be sterile and to be a reporter of sorts, but not an educator who is creative and provocative.

The cast of characters who inform every area of human knowledge must not only be women as well as men, but must include women and men of minority races as well as the majority race; must include the economically impoverished; the workers in the vineyards of the home, the factory, the hotels, the laundries, the marketplaces, the hospitals, the churches, the offices, the community, the neighborhood, the public housing, the farms and the villages. Not only must this wider cast of characters inform and educate students and teachers about human affairs and our environments, but responsible academia must be informed and educated *about* and by the lives, the thoughts, the home life, the art, the music, the humor, the language, the lifestyles, the families, the health, the aspirations, the values, the spirituality, the achievements, the problems, the strengths and the myths about those generally excluded from academia. Many of the excluded are the genuine educators.

Those excluded are the underclasses of women, of minority peoples, of the poor, of homosexual people, of people with handicaps. These are at least 75% of the U.S. population. We somehow arrange survival or finesse survival hazards, and have some of the most holistic/universal visions to generate and sustain change movements. Visions have no precedent, no documented "validity," no background of scholarship, but surely visions do have political implications – as do existing scholarship and disciplines. Those with consciousness changed from the predominant but limited consciousness have the insights to see the educational value and potential of new studies and new perspectives on older studies. It is time to move feminism and other significant change movements from the margins and peripheral areas to the center, to create the paradigm shifts and wholeness which are the quests of humanity.

NOTES

1. Indeed, for fascinating and provocative history, read Historian Linda Gordon, who works on understanding history from the bottom up, not the top down. She documents and chronicles the lives of women and others not considered or expected to be powerful but who influenced history anyway, eg, *Women's Body, Women's Right*, a social history of birth control in America, Penguin Books, 1977.

2. Ephron, Nora: *Crazy Salad, Some Things About Women*. Alfred Knopf, New York. 1975.

3. Baker, Liva: *I'm Radcliffe, Fly Me: The Seven Sisters and the Failure of Women's Education*. Macmillan, New York. 1976.

4. Hubbard, Ruth: "With Will to Choose." *Harvard Crimson*. October 19, 1976.

5. Collins, Shelia: *A Different Heaven and Earth*. Judson Press, Valley Forge, PA 1974.

6. Broverman, I., S. Vogel, D. Broverman, F. Clarkson, P. Rosencrantz: "Sex Role Stereotypes: A Current Appraisal." *Journal of Social Issues*. Vol. 28, 1972, pp. 59-78.

7. Heide, Wilma Scott: "Testimony on H.R. 9030: Better Income and Jobs (sic)." *Record of Hearings on Legislation*, 1977.

8. Russell, Michelle: "An Open Letter to The Academy." *Quest: A Feminist Quarterly.* Spring 1977. 3:4. pp. 70-80. Special issue on race, class and culture.

9. At this point, I raise an unanswerable question: If white women had not been devalued and subjugated, if "feminine" values hadn't been devalued and privatized as if for women only, would the white man have enslaved the Black people? Since we cannot relive history, we'll never know, but my response is "probably not." That does not erase white women's general complicity, but it raises a question still relevant to today's racism and sexism in higher education and society.

10. Did you know Elizabeth Cady Stanton had a brilliant sense of humor? Would Bach have been such a prolific composer if he had had a child every year from the age of 16 (as did his wife) and been responsible for their care without his spouse contributing at all? It is women who create, design and weave the magnificent "Persian" rugs. Did you know that? I didn't until recently.

11. Harris, Ann Sutherland and Linda Nochlin: *Women Artists: 1550-1950.* Alfred A. Knopf, New York. 1976. Also, the first international exhibition of works by women artists at the Brooklyn Museum, October 1-November 27, 1977.

12. Roszak, Betty and Theodore: *Masculine/Feminine: Readings in Sexual Mythology and the Liberation of Women.* Harper and Row, New York. 1969.

13. *Signs: A Journal of Women in Culture and Society.* Published by the University of Chicago Press.

14. Carmichael, Carrie: *Non-Sexist Childraising.* Beacon, Boston. 1977.

15. Hochchild, Arlie Russell: "The Sociology of Feeling and Emotion: Selected Possibilities." In Marcia Millman and Rosabeth Moss Kanter (Eds.) *Another Voice: Feminist Perspectives on Social Life and Social Service.* Anchor Press/Doubleday, New York. 1975. pp. 280-307.

16. Boulding, Elise: *The Underside of History: A View of Women Through Time, Including Futurist Recommendations.* Westview Press, Boulder, CO. 1976.

17. Roberts, Joan (Ed.): *Beyond Intellectual Sexism: A New Woman, A New Reality.* David McKay Co., New York. 1976.

18. Rich, Adrienne: "Toward a Woman-Centered University." In Florence Howe (Ed.) *Women and the Power to Change.* McGraw Hill, New York. 1975. This essay also appears in Adrienne Rich's book *On Lies, Secrets and Silence.* W.W. Norton, New York. 1979.

19. Gilligan, Carol: "In a Different Voice: Women's Conceptions of Self and of Morality." *Harvard Educational Review.* 47:4, November 1977. pp. 481-516. Also see Carol Gilligan's book *In a Different Voice: Psychological Theory and Women's Development.* Harvard University Press, Cambridge, MA 1982.

20. 'Actor' is a generic word referring to people of both sexes. I do not accept allegedly female derivative terms like 'actress'.

21. *The American College Dictionary.* Random House, New York. 1963.

22. Gould, Carol C: "Philosophy of Liberation and the Liberation of Philosophy." In Carol C. Gould and Mark Warofsky (Eds.): *Women and Philosophy: Toward a Theory of Liberation.* G.P. Putnam's Sons, New York. 1975. pp. 5-44.

    Interestingly and disappointingly, Professor Gould partly fails her own criterion for critical philsophy by using *he, his* and *him* (clearly male-only pronouns) as if they were each a generic reference (for humans of both sexes) in her otherwise useful analysis of philosophy. She does include a delineation of how semi-versal (my term), would-be philosophy distorts the essential nature of first principles, of universality, of knowledge, of understanding the human condition and human affairs. Philosophy Professor Gertrude Ezorsky succinctly states the problem: "Where the concepts are biased, the precepts are blind." (in "Hiring Women Faculty." *Philosophy and Public Affairs.* 7:1, September, 1977.)

23. Harris, William H. and Judith S. Levey (Eds.): *The New Columbia Encyclopedia.* Columbia University Press, New York. 1975.

24. Daly, Mary: *Beyond God The Father: Toward a Philosophy of Women's Liberation.* Beacon, Boston. 1973.

25. Mendelsohn, Everett: "A Human Reconstruction of Science." In *Women: A Resource for a Changing World* (Radcliffe Institute Symposium). *Boston University Journal.* 21:2. Spring, 1973.

26. The word 'defend' is military and adversarial language – the word 'embody' is preferable.

27. Arditti, Rita: "Women in Science: 'Women Drink Water While Men Drink Wine'." *Science for the People.* 8:2. March, 1976. pp. 24-26.

28. Sullivan, Dan: "The Arrogance of Male Power." *Jubilee.* December 1967. Vol. 15. pp. 24-25.

29. Heide, Wilma Scott: "A Feminist's Perspective on Manipulation of Woman (Woman includes Man)." In *The Genetic Manipulation of Man [sic] Symposium.* Proceedings of the Symposium at Stevens Point, University of Wisconsin. November 8, 1973. p. 5. Available from KNOW, INC. P.O. Box 86031, Pittsburgh, PA 15221.

30. Arditti, Rita, Renate Duelli Klein and Shelly Minden (Eds.): *Test-Tube Women.* Pandora Press, 9 Park St., Boston, MA 02108. 1984. The Editors note: "We have to look carefully at how much real choice reproductive technologies offer to women."

31. Women's Educational Resources. "Women's Work – Up From 878." *Report on the Dictionary of Occupational Titles Research Project.* University of Wisconsin Extension, 610 Langden St., Madison, WI 53706. 1975.

32. Macoby, Eleanor and Carol Jacklin: *The Psychology of Sex Differences.* Stanford University Press, Stanford, CA 1975.

33. As a functioning behavioral research scientist, I know that research differences studies are more easily funded than sex similarities studies by those who hold the purse strings. So much for objectivity. I asked Jacklin in 1976 if she and Macoby ever considered titling their book *The Psychology of Sex Similarities.* She said they had not and acknowledged research funds for sex similarities would have been more difficult to obtain.

34. Griffiths, Dorothy and Esther Saraga: "Sex Differences in Cognitive Abilities: A Sterile Field of Enquiry?" *Women Speaking.* October 1977. 4:3. pp. 4-8. Paper first given at British Psychological Society in July 1977.

35. Gilligan, John: "Women – An Important But Neglected Resource." *Front Lines* [note military language] Agency for International Development, U.S. State Department, Washington, D.C. Note that this quote does not acknowledge the fact that men are also being trained in the new agricultural technologies, leaving women to bear as well as rear the children, as well as do the housework and maintain the village, etc., etc. I would also add that the planners themselves must *be* women, not simply give women an equal place.

36. Leghorn, Lisa and Mary Roodkowsky: *Who Really Starves? Women and World Hunger.* Friendship Press in cooperation with Church World Service, 475 Riverside Dr. New York. 1977. Also see Hosken, Fran P. (Ed.): "Women and Food." *WINews, Women's International Network.* 4:1, pp. 20-30. Available from Women's International Network, 187 Grant St., Lexington, MA 02173.

37. *World Agricultural Research Project.* Department of Population Sciences, School of Public Health, Harvard University, 665 Huntington Ave., Boston, MA 02115. From the Introduction to and Summary (to date) of the Project.

38. Hacker, Sally: "Farming Out The Home: Women and Agribusiness." *The Second Wave.* Spring/Summer 1977, 5:1, pp. 38-49.

39. Rosenman, Mark: *A Discussion of Higher Education as Socialization and Social-Economic Political Control: Programmatic Implications for Social Change and Individual Development.* Unpublished PhD Dissertation. 1976. Author at Campus Free College, 2025 I St. NW, Washington, D.C. 20006.

40. Bird, Caroline: *The Case Against College.* David McKay Co., New York. 1975.

CHAPTER TWO

FEMINISM:
MAKING A DIFFERENCE IN OUR HEALTH

When one is writing about interrelated phenomena, the matter of sequence generally arises. So too, in my decision to place the chapter on education and knowledge before this chapter on health; though the former may be literally academic without the latter in individual lives. I placed the matters of knowledge and education first, because these chapters are "think pieces," and I hope the criticizing and degendering of conventional knowledge and education will facilitate reconceptualizations of health care. This chapter will focus on some of the contributions of feminism to health care and a few of my visions of the differences feminism will make for wholistic health care.

Sexism is splitting the world and its people, the male-generated medical model of health care is dangerous to our health in the wholistic sense. Feminism as a healing reformulation by nurturance of the human body and spirit, (which is born whole, is the generic imperative for health care. Medicines, surgery and instrumentation can dramatically augment health care, but nursing – nurturance and nourishment of the whole person – is the crucial element of health care. It is women who are currently most in touch with nurturance and care. People of both sexes who value these "feminine" qualities are most qualified to lead in a redefinition and restructuring of health care itself. Feminist values are fundamental to creating the healing difference in our individual and societal health.

"What would happen if one woman told the truth about her life? The *world* would split open."[1,p.xi] Women by the millions *are* telling the truths about our lives, including the truth about our health care. As a result it may seem to some that the world and health care therein is being irreversibly split open. Increasing feminist consciousness and actions *reveal* the already existing split from existing artificial dichotomies consequent to sexism in health care. Women's experience in health care reveals how womankind has been made into an artificial object and depowered. Marge Piercy depicts women's oppression well in her poem "A Work of Artifice." The poem compares the artificial prunning of the bonsai tree with the stunting of the growth of women by foot binding, brain crippling, curling of hair, and valuing "the hands you love to touch."[2,p.3]

Perceptive poets, feminists, health activists have more wholistic visions of people not artificially split by mind and body, objective and subjective, rational and emotional, cure and care, "masculine" and "feminine." A newborn infant arrives whole, not split by these dualities. The newborn could remain whole, through our rejection of the idea of patriarchy and its consequent splits and dualities. Patriarchy has created these dualisms consequent to the male's frequent alienation from his body, his learned denial of subjective and emotional validity, his delegating of care to people subordinate (usually women), and his learned denial of his "feminine" qualities as well as his denial of the "masculine" qualities of women. The alienations and dualisms of patriarchy have devastated true health care. Feminism rejects and transcends these bifurcations of people and values, and promotes the retention of newborn wholeness. Feminism portends the reconciliation and healing of people and of the artificial split of the world which feminist articulation has merely revealed, not caused.

Increasingly influenced by feminist consciousness, nurses are rejecting the handmaiden role and are assertively redefining the nurse as a leader who may best guide the total care of the whole patient. In this changing context, physicians are seen as highly trained technicians prepared for instrumental roles – not the sole decision makers. As nurses and nursing become more powerful and as men become more liberated from sex stereotyping, the health occupations will become increasingly gender integrated. Fundamentally, the feminist redefinition of power – enabling the self to *be* and *become* and *not* to control others – portends qualitative changes in the legal, ethical and personal relationships among health providers and with their clients/patients.

Definitions of Health Care

Definitions of health care can be profoundly influenced by feminism. From my perspective, health care is essentially an interrelational phenomenon that may be augmented by chemical and physical technologies. In the current medical model, instrumental technology and the relative overvaluing of procedures and techniques that are performed on passive people have often dominated the qualitative, expressive components of care. Feminism has generated ideals that transcend any medicine, surgery and/or physiotherapy. Feminist values provide the experiential reality whereby health care encounters are affectively positive, conducive to healing and nurturing of positive self-images for both clients and practitioners.

Feminists and others have noted the deification of the M.D. in our culture. In regards to what I call the M.D.eity, Wildavsky states:

> According to the great equation, available medical care equals health, but the great equation is wrong. More available medical care alone does not equal health. The best estimates are that the medical system itself affects about 10% of the usual indices for measuring health, ie, whether you live, how well you live, how long you live. The remaining 90% are determined by factors over which doctors have little or no control: such as individual life style, social conditions, and the physical environment.[3,p.105]

Most of the bad things that happen to people are at present beyond the reach of medicine. This is not to say that medicine is good for nothing - only that it is not good for everything.

Although most knowledgeable people realize that the "great equation" is wrong and that medical care determines only a small proportion of health indicators, physicians still have most of the power in the system. Health policy decisions are made in the context of a value system that is white, androcentric and capitalist. The typical medical center and many hospitals resemble the capitalist business enterprise in values and sometimes in profits; an unconscionable condition.

Feminism portends deprofiteering of health practice and greater emphasis on preventative care. While not all physicians are profit-oriented, it is still true that disease is most profitable to physicians and more profitable than preventative practice. Medical technologies representing the instrumental approach to problem-solving are funded at the expense of the expressive approach of interrelationships and social technologies. Personal and social factors represent 90% of health indices that determine the underlying health status of people: housing, nutrition, fair employment opportunities, humane interrelationships, a single standard of mental health for both sexes, realization of social and economic justice. Much of this nurturance and expressiveness reflects subordinated values toward which primarily women have been socialized and privatized. The instrumental, mechanized, physical, chemical and dominant approach represents the values toward which primarily men have been socialized – and these have been made to seem and become the predominant public "values" – including those of health policy.

Feminist values free both sexes to express their positive aspects of both feminine and masculine behaviors, opening the possibility to apply feminine values in public policy. The potential of this value re-orientation in health policy alone is virtually immeasurable, partly because not all qualitative factors can be quantified. The idea that every phenomenon can be quantified is itself an essentially male-derived bias. Quantification is related to the proclivity to control people and nature.

As of 1970, physicians and administrators (mostly men) comprised only 12% of the health workforce, whereas in the 19th century physicians alone accounted for 52% of the paid health workforce. Policy-making power has not been proportionately dispersed, only the work has been dispersed – and most of that work (88%) is done by women of all races and minority men.[4] Thus, a fraction of the health workforce controls the recognized intellectual and planning dimensions of the work.

While not natural, such controlling results are predictable in cultures and societies where sex dimorphism and consequent gender role learning related to sex are the norm. This is especially true if a society is androcentric. Male socialization usually emphasizes self-interest, self-development, self-achievement and self-power over others. This is compounded by female socialization to care for and nurture others, and suppression of her self-interest, self-achievement and frequent eschewing of power, even over her own body and life. Feminism is making a positive difference in societal and individual health by demystifying knowledge, self-help and promoting political activism leading to changed consciousness.

Demystification

The implications of feminist reorientations of all health care are profound. Feminist consciousness demystifies important knowledge and rejects condescending attitudes toward women, as well as toward the poor and the ethnic and social minorities. The practitioner who explains the treatment of a woman only to her husband or another male or feels threatened by clients who insist on participating in care, must be re-educated.

In order to begin radical demystification, feminists are proposing that:

- only women be admitted to the practice of obstetrics and gynecology,
- no additional monies be awarded to men for research of female reproduction,
- an independent commission (in essence feminists) to administer any laws concerning female reproduction, abortion and sterilization and remove jurisdiction from patriarchal courts and legislative systems,
- and that "the United Nations and United States will not sponsor nor participate in any international population activity or conference unless women are represented in proportion to their numbers in the population of every participating nation."[5,p.44]

Barbara Seaman, one who proposes this states: "It may be a most basic violation of civil rights for the group that is not at any risk from reproduction (male) to control the group that is at risk (female)."[5,p.45] Biologist Rita Arditti makes a powerful case for the crucial need to re-educate men about their responsibilities and opportunities regarding reproduction, contraceptives and sexuality. She documents the sexual politics of the existing research establishment and the profit motive of the drug industry as potent barriers to a safe, simple and effective contraceptive for *either* sex for the next few years.[6]

Eighty-six percent of women enter the health system and services via their reproductive organs[7] because the male-dominated American Medical Association (AMA) organizes woman's health care around her uterus and her reproductive potential.[8] Indeed, the AMA would have the obstretrician-gynecologist (mostly men) formally recognized as women's primary health providers.[9]

As long as the obstretics-gynecology specialties exist, limiting entrance to women-only until men are re-educated is supportable, and would not be a violation of the (ultimately) ratified Equal Rights Amendment.[10] However, Helen Marieskind's proposal to re-evaluate and eliminate the specialties themselves suggests a more radical and even healthier prospect. Marieskind observes that "not only the practices and content of obstetrics-gynecology are often oppressive to women but the *very* concept of a reproductively-oriented specialty by the medical system reinforces the social ideology that views women as sex objects and reproductive organs. Women need health care that acknowledges we are 'whole persons, not an isolated ovary or uterus to be controlled.'"[8,p.49]

Self-Help Movements

Self-help organizations are vital to the women's health movement. They involve *assertive nurturance* based on the discovery and sharing of knowledge and skills so that women and men can create their own health destinies.

Feminist Women's Health Centers[11] are in the forefront of the self-help movement. Other important self-help modalities that are not frankly feminist have developed around the country and often work with or as agents of feminist change. The self-help movement reflects and generates certain values that are themselves therapeutic – including the self-confidence to help oneself and others. The movement also focuses on acquiring the skills to do so. The processes require active contributions instead of – or in addition to – passive reception. Self-help is based on the principle that one can learn something by being prepared to teach it. Persuading others first requires self-persuasion and involvement. One thus gains self-confidence, strength and health.

The professional model of care emphasizes cognitive knowledge – an instrumental approach – and "objectivity" in relation to patients. It also involves systematic and standardized approaches, a controlled environment, the promise of cure (at least of symptoms) and a fee for service.

The aprofessional self-help model includes cognitive knowledge but emphasizes the intuitive and experiential, spontaneity and identification with the consumer. It often is free or the fee is based on a sliding scale and its techniques are less visibly circumscribed. It emphasizes the total person. Although both approaches overlap, the relative emphases are important. The feminist approach is closer to the self-help aprofessional model. It therapeutically empowers the consumer/patient and attempts to diminish hierarchies of control and power. Since professional expertise can be a resource, an important goal is to make this expertise nonauthoritarian.

While the self-help potential for health care is an important force, especially in a capitalist society, there are political risks. These risks become critical if support for self-help allows public services to be funded inadequately or if it lets national leaders "off the hook" with respect to their responsibilities to fund health and other important public services. There is also the risk that needed public services will only be provided in lifesaving or emergency situations and that self-help will be relegated to those problems that have traditionally been blamed on the victims, thereby avoiding societal responsibility to remove the institutional causations of problems.

Political Activism

The National Women's Health Network monitors and works to influence national health policy, provides a clearinghouse and serves an action-generative function that avoids overpersonalization and regionalism. In 1977 a bimonthly academic journal, *Women and Health*,[12] was initiated by the National Women's Health Network. The burgeoning of feminist research on health and other human issues portends new insights and potential for unbiased, human problem-solving.

Organized for action in 1973, one task force of the National Organization for Women, Inc. (NOW), was Nurses NOW.[13] One purpose of Nurses NOW was to reflect feminist awareness that organizations, including hospitals, need to be organized horizontally rather than vertically in order to end the unhealthy pecking order of practical nurses, aides and orderlies. These groups are even more oppressed than (and sometimes by) professional nurses as well as physicians.

In February 1974, I met with the American Nurses' Association Board of Directors to carry strong messages and a challenge from Nurses NOW; to encourage the ANA to change their ostensibly apolitical position on certain issues and to acknowledge the political nature and multiple consequences of sexism for nursing and health care. The primary issue was not whether to be political. To be ostensibly apolitical is to choose, by acts of omission, to accept sexist politics. Choosing feminist politics would be corrective and affirmative acts of commission.

In May 1974, the ANA formed a political arm, Nurses' Coalition for Action in Politics (N-CAP), reportedly a response to our February meeting. Among other programs, N-CAP monitors, keeps score, lobbies legislators and legislation and works to support or replace legislators – depending on their actions. In three key 1975 congressional votes on health and nursing issues, the ANA N-CAP positions were upheld.[14] Some state nursing associations have formed political action committees. The increasing politicizing of nurses, the largest profession of women (mostly) may yet be recognized as a major public health measure.

Changed Consciousness

Action to change consciousness occurs as women insist on participation in public policy-making organizations. For example, the National Institute of Health (NIH) has been pressed to include more women in public advisory, research and administrative functions. Prior to 1972 less than 10% of these positions were filled by women, although women comprise over 75% of health care providers and over 50% of health care users. Sustained attempts to produce change were not persuasive until a 1972 lawsuit began to effect some results.[15] The lawsuit was initiated by a coalition of organizations including the NOW Legal Defense and Education Fund and fifteen individual plaintiffs including myself. NIH finally began to "beat the bushes" to get women in advisory, research and administrative positions (after much legal maneuvering to avoid doing so) and increased the numbers of women re-actively, but still not pro-actively, feminist.

In addition to books, articles and pamphlets, the creative involvement of the new media indicates that a dynamic development of changed consciousness has occurred. The film, *Taking Our Bodies Back*[16] brilliantly explores ten critical areas of the women's health movement from revolutionary self-help concepts to informed surgical consent. The need for more women to participate in public policy about health care was communicated. The film also documented the action of feminists who generated concerted action on the double standard in health care, psychosurgery abuses, drug misuse, corporate drug companies' malpractices, nutrition and malnutrition, genetic manipulation, insurance practices and industrial health.

Mental Health Issues

A double standard of mental health has been well documented.[17,18,19] Newer data overwhelmingly document the charges, but problems continue to exist in the mental health field. Those who deviate from standards of "appropriate" feminine or masculine behavior are considered abnormal, unnatural and sick. "Masculine" behavior is valued by mental health practitioners more highly than "feminine" behavior. "Masculine" behavior is considered virtually synonymous with "normal" behavior for mature adults. "Feminine" behavior, while considered "ideal" for allegedly mature females, is seen as immature for adults. Those who deviate have been, and still may be, exposed to therapists who try to adjust them.

An example of the abuses of the virtually powerless by the relatively powerful is found in the area of psychosurgery. These procedures were discredited in the late 1940's as being both ineffective and irreversible. Many critics felt that patients were victimized by powerful physicians. While psychosurgery was labeled therapy, it was clearly experimentation.

One major group of subjects was women. The goals of the "treatment" were to eliminate or modify aggressive behavior supposedly not responsive to other methods. The treatment was deemed "successful" if treated women returned to passive "femininity" willingly performing housekeeping and homemaker "duties." The absence of consent, informed or otherwise; the lack of understanding by these subjects, who were already confined in institutions often against their will, were also causes for protest.

A moratorium on psychosurgery did result in 1973 only after Joan Goldstein (NOW Health Task Force Coordinator) and I met with the Director of the National Institute of Mental Health (NIMH) to demand it. NIMH was funding psychosurgery with *public money*. Eternal vigilance appears to be necessary. In 1977 the federal government again allocated funds for lobotomies for a project whose primary "target" was white middle-class, middle-aged women.[20]

It is the ideas and the idealizers of superimposed adjustments for either sex who require adjustment, therapy and education.[21] The Association for Women in Psychology[22] along with other feminists in psychiatry, sociology, social work and nursing, is providing leadership in the healthy re-orientation of mental health practitioners and society. This feminist education is a significant public health measure which the tax-monied NIMH earlier eschewed but to which it is now beginning to respond positively. Efforts are being made in many fields to educate our colleagues and society to a single standard of mental health for both sexes.

Corporate Drug Malpractice

The tragic case of corporate malpractice can be seen in the use of the Dalkon Shield, an intrauterine device (IUD) that was removed from the market in 1975 after evidence mounted regarding its harmful effects and protests increased from feminists and others.[23] Seventeen women had died from its use before 1976, and countless others suffered severe infection. Those who profited from its sale were never prosecuted until the late '70's and the early '80's. Finally, in 1984 even the offending corporation, A.H. Robins Co. was pressed to take some responsibility by asking Dalkon Shield users to contact them using a toll-free number (1-800-247-7220). At the corporation's expense, users can now receive aid and removal of the Dalkon shields.

The need for monitoring and constraining is illustrated by the problems arising from the use of diethylstilbestrol (DES). Beginning in the 1940's, DES was prescribed to pregnant women to prevent miscarriages. By 1960 the effectiveness of DES was questioned and many physicians stopped using it. In January 1973, the federal Food and Drug Administration (FDA) banned the use of DES in cattle feed, judging the ".00003 mgs. remaining in beef to be carcinogenic for human consumption."[24] In March 1975 the FDA approved the use of DES in a 250 mg dose in human women for use as a postcoital contraceptive, or "morning after pill," in "emergency situations." Left to the physicians' discretions were decisions about what constitutes an emergency and of informing patients of possible side effects to the fetus, should the drug be ineffective; and of the possible carcinogenic effects with long-term use. By April 1975 some daughters of DES-treated women had developed vaginal cancer, a cancer rare in this age group.

It had been estimated that 80% of the DES daughters will have adenosis, which is an abnormal form of vaginal cellular development which may be a precursor of cancer. There is now an incontestable chain of evidence linking DES given to pregnant women with the possible appearance of adenocarcinoma in their daughters.[25, p.6]

Nutrition, Malnutrition and Hunger

Drug and pharmaceutical corporations, the food industry, agribusiness firms, multi-national corporations and physicians' practices are being challenged by feminists and others as food activists. The reasons include:

- corporate practices and prices exacerbate hunger and malnutrition especially in poor countries;[26]
- poor nutrition is fostered in the United States, including public school lunch programs and exported worldwide by fast-food chains like MacDonalds;[27]
- the great failure of medical schools to pay much attention to the science of nutrition.[28]

It is ironic that with women as the major food growers, processors, preparers and feeders in most countries of the world, men are considered the experts, near exclusive policymakers and – not surprisingly – exploiters. Woman, the nurturer by conditioning if not by nature, has second-hand tools (if any) and poorer nutrition. Hunger and malnutrition, the greatest causes of irreversible brain damage and growth deficiencies in the young, are visited twice as much on girls as on boys in the United States alone.[29] Boys are simply more valued than girls.[30,31] When food, especially proteins are scarce, males are given preference. Can any one doubt the positive difference in health of all, especially girls and women, as feminists move from micro-politics of nutrition to macro-politics as well?

Genetic Manipulation and Research

Whether rejecting sexist nutrition policies and practices at home and abroad or while moving on micro-politics and macro-politics of sickness and health, feminists are aware that rejecting sexist ideology of much medical teaching and practice must include the important areas of genetic research, manipulation and sterilization. The demographic characteristics of the genetics researchers influence their judgments. Ethical issues are raised by genetic research and manipulation. Genetics is *not* value free, nor is any other area of science and health care. This work occurs in a political and socioeconomic context. Genetic research, policy and practice do not begin or end with the intrauterine life of the embryo. The allocation of health research funds is profoundly influenced by politics in both the generic and partisan senses.

Though apparently little known (yet) to the general public or even the scientific and health communities, feminists of varied credentials *are* articulating our perspectives, insights and concerns around genetic engineering and possible genetic manipulation; about the demographics of the researcher population; about the criteria in cost accounting and cost benefit ratios in genetics' policies; about the political consciousness of policymakers; about the ethical issues in cloning and gene construction; and about how the funding for research on the relatively few potentially "defective" unborns is sanctified "while the huge human drama of the disanctity of much human life of the already born goes systematically almost untouched."[32]

In 1984 a feminist national and international Network on the New Reproductive Technologies formed. Janice Raymond of Women's Studies at the University (Semi-versity) of Massachusetts in Amherst, Massachusetts is the U.S. contact. The technology has enormous implications for women, is controlled (currently) by men and "masculine" values. It seems that some men are now intent on getting into the "baby-making" business beyond being sperm donors. Their approach appears to be instrumental and mechanical. Womb envy is a wondrous and surely androcentric, worrisome phenomenon. Feminists are appropriately wary, critical, and becoming organized on these issues.[33]

Insurance Practices and Industrial Health Policies

Changes are needed in financing health care. Much of the sexism in health insurance is due to mythology, such as the inaccurate information that women's absenteeism is greater than men's. Feminists are changing laws and insisting on equitable compliance with laws by civil rights enforcement agencies themselves.

In 1973 the Equal Employment Opportunity Commission (EEOC) was prepared to accept the notion that, since women generally outlive men, all women should receive less retirement benefits per month or year than men. I reminded the Commissioners that since white people generally outlive black people, it follows that white people should receive lower benefits than black people. The EEOC could see their inconsistency and double standard. However, our promise of a mandamus action (a legal action to assure that a public agency performs its legislated responsibilities) if they did not advance the policy of equitable benefits, accompanied by media attention on their sexism were necessary to persuade the EEOC to enforce the laws.[34]

This action was welcomed by people of color of both sexes whose racist disadvantages are prime causes of their shorter lives. Feminists have and do work(ed) in coalitions with other civil rights and health activists much more than the general media have reported.[35]

Other coalitions of feminists in and with unions, civil rights and economic justice organizations are acting to insure industrial health, safety and opportunity for all workers. Some women are presently excluded from certain occupations that are deemed by others to be dangerous to our health – particularly if we are pregnant. These working conditions are hazardous to men as well. The work situation should be changed for all, rather than "protecting" women to an extent that excludes us from opportunities.[36] In very real ways, women need most to protect ourselves from self-appointed protectors and policy-makers for whom life as a woman is a foreign affair.

International Programs and Possibilities

After pressure by feminists, 1975-1985 was declared the International Woman's Decade by the United Nations, although the U.N. denies that they responded to pressure in doing so. Consequently, in 1977 the United States issues and problems of women were addressed in state-wide conferences and at a subsequent National conference to follow up the International Women's Year (IWY) conference in Mexico in 1975. Four major health areas were considered: 1) health rights, 2) health literacy,

3) access to quality care and 4) women as health providers and consumers. The IWY commission report of 1976 made recommendations in health research, policy, economics, drug abuse, alcohol, cancer, training, mental health, consciousness raising and women's assertiveness training.[37] The implementation of these recommendations would be major gains, and may become possible as increasing numbers of feminists enter policy-making positions.

Looking at the picture in a few other nations, some few examples of the dangers of sexism to female health will indicate why feminism is so imperative for the health of it. In India, women and girls generally receive fewer resources than males. It is the practice among some groups for wife, mother and girls to eat only after males of all ages have eaten, and then only whatever is left; marriage and childbearing occur as young as ten years for girls; less education, if any, is available for girls than boys; and the "neglect and maltreatment of women by society, in-laws or husbands after marriage affects their emotional and mental health."[38] India is not alone in its misogyny.

Internationally feminists have taken independent actions on health issues in other countries. For example, Fran P. Hosken has been campaigning almost alone to end the genital mutilation of girls (as young as four years) and women in Africa by infibulation, circumcision, excision and/or clitoridectomy. These procedures cause many physical and psychological problems and even death. The purposes of the procedure are to assure chastity, virginity and females' reduced sexual response. Although part of an entire cultural pattern, the decisions are made by and for men. Growing documentation of these cruel and inhumane practices, tortures and oppressions demonstrate denial of most basic human rights. Yet, the U.S. State Departments will take no action and even grant millions of dollars for countries that use *this* money to perpetuate these obscenities.[39] There are some who view these practices, however painful and/or deadly, as merely local or national customs, and for the U.S. to object or intervene, to be U.S. cultural imperialism. If that be cultural imperialism, we (the U.S.) should cease *all* mutual defense (offense?) pacts with other countries when merely oil, copper, tin, zinc or men's lives are in danger. The continued double standard vis-à-vis intervention/nonintervention is misogynous and intolerable.

Health needs of women in many parts of the world beg for feminist perspectives and actions. One example is the pressures on poor women in developing countries to spend their limited resources on bottle feeding and on prepared baby foods, rather than rely on breast feeding. This pressure is applied by U.S. multi-national corporations that exploit the actual or functional illiteracy of many women so that they spend scarce funds to bottle-feed their infants when breast feeding is more efficient, safer, healthier and more economical. Political activism finally changed the behavior of Nestle Corporation, but never did persuade Ronald Reagan and his white male club (in orientation) that this was an issue important enough for them to support.

In March 1976, feminists around the world organized an International Tribunal on Crimes against Women, including crimes by the medical profession.[40] Over 2,000 women from 40 countries came to Belgium to bear witness to just a sample of the world's misogyny. This Tribunal was a non-governmental follow-up to the World's First International Feminist planning conference convened by NOW, in Cambridge, Massachusetts in June 1973.[41] The Tribunal was five electrifying days of accounts by women speaking out publicly, individually and at personal risk about heretofore private crimes against women.

Reproductive Choice

Increasingly, around the world, a familiar demand of feminists is for people to control our own bodies and for self-determined reproductive choices. This includes contraception, abortion and voluntary sterilization. It is the right of the woman (who still bears the major daily consequences of completed pregnancy) to determine whether or not she will bear children. In a world where millions starve each year, compulsory pregnancy is obscene. This issue is especially compelling in the context of the fact that in two hours, the world spends on armaments what it spends in one year on children.[42] Women inform these priorities almost not at all.

Women are beginning to decide if, when and *how* to have babies. The resurgence of midwifery promises to de-medicalize childbirth, recognize the woman giving birth as the significant actor, and relate to childbirth as an essentially natural process. Control of our bodies, including reproductive choices and childbirth practices, is neither possible nor adequate until women redefine power and share leadership and control of health and other social institutions.

Knowledge – its identification, its definition, its sharing – is power, especially for those who define what is considered knowledge. As the power of traditional organized patriarchal religion wanes somewhat in more educated circles, overmedicalization of society plays a key role as the source and enforcer of institutional sexism, through medical teaching as if it were scientific fact. Medical knowledge begins with conception, literally and intellectually. Knowledge of female reproductive physiology is distorted by the androcentric lens that projects male fantasy onto female functions. The sperm travels to the ovum not by reason of its motile flagellum, as current "scientific" journals and literary imaginings allege, but by virtue of female oxytocin which produces uterine contractions that propel the sperm. Indeed, completely inert substances such as dead sperm and particles of India ink reach the oviducts as rapidly as live sperm do. So much for the mythology of a powerful "active" sperm and a passive waiting ovum in one more bit of "male sexual imagery structuring the very act of conception."[43] Small wonder we advocate feminist schools of medicine and women's health schools.[44,45]

Women and men share a transcending humanity, yet women and men are not biologically identical in structure, in physiology and potential reproductive functions. To suggest that even revolutionary menstrual extraction, self-abortions, test-tube conception and laboratory breeding in lieu of human pregnancy will eliminate biological differences between the sexes may represent a non-conscious implied acceptance of the predicted primacy of androcentric technocracy.[43, p.26]

Yet our different bodies, our particular biologies and physiologies are not the central issues. The central issues are the *definitions* of our biology, the control of our bodies and health care, and the values and value-holders that define and interpret what is immutable biology and what is culturally learned and valued. The issue of power is intrinsic to the knowledge, to the technology developed, to extant health care. The medical system that dominates health practice is not only a "service" industry. It is a powerful institution and basis for social control, particularly of women especially by men. It is profoundly pathological that what is called "health care" is (currently) primarily dominated by those (physicians) whose training is oriented to disease and medicine – *not* health care.

Reformulations of Health Care and Future Visions

Jean Baker Miller makes some important observations:

> ... in the course of projecting into women's domain some of its most troublesome and problematic exigencies male-led society may also have simultaneously, and unwittingly, delegated to women not humanity's "lowest needs" but its "highest necessities" – that is, the intense, emotionally connected cooperation

and creativity necessary for human life and growth. Further, it is women who today perceive that they must openly and consciously demand them if they are to achieve even the beginnings of personal integrity.[46,p.25-26]

Miller asserts that women have filled in these necessities without portfolio, with little societal support, and even without the dominant culture substantively acknowledging these as essentials or recognizing women's creativity. She correctly emphasizes the strengths of women performing humanity's highest necessities.

Miller identifies what women have done, what men can learn, and what feminists are demanding as more advanced forms of thinking, relating and working. Women are not only discovering qualities that are strengths and their devaluing as weaknesses to be oppressive, but are also beginning to refuse to be what I call unilateral emotional jockstraps for men. This is and will press men to confront their vulnerabilities, their periodic helplessness and emotionality, and thus strengthen many fragile male egos, a prophecy I consider to have healthy potential.

Could it be that the over 50% of people who have no organic problem or dysfunction turn to physicians for some of the "higher necessities" for which most physicians are unprepared to provide? Could it also be that a large portion of the 90% of factors that determine health and its qualitative indicators are made up of the individual and institutional arrangements for these higher necessities – or the absence of such arrangements? I think so.

Imagine the stunning possibilities of reformulating health-care values, and thus policies based on realities of human needs and humane priorities. Nutritional, social, environmental, economic, legal, human service, knowledge accuracy and sharing factors could receive the bulk of the actual health-care resources. The 10% of health factors which physicians, drugs and technologies can influence therapeutically would augment, not control, health care. For this to happen, feminist consciousness and actions must become cultural realities – valuing women as well as men and valuing many "feminine" (virtually synonymous with humane) qualities of women and men privately and publicly.

WHAT IF feminism were used as a healing process to de-hierarchalize current health practices? As nurturance, as the "feminine" strengths, as the higher necessities of Jean Baker Miller's formulations become valued, power itself would be redefined in the health care system. I think this will represent a more mature perception of psychosocial development, of interrelationships, of leadership in health practice. Oppression itself and/or suppression of positive aspects of "femininity" or "masculinity" for either sex are all unhealthy. Power used to control others, rather than to facilitate empowerment and thus the health of others, would become disqualifications for health practice.

WHAT IF corrective and wholistic women's studies were required for all practicing health care providers? These studies would focus on eliminating sexist health concepts, policies and practices. Futurist feminist studies would be required parts of curricula for all future health practitioners, ultimately eliminating the need for corrective studies.

WHAT IF sexist language were eliminated from health care? The elimination of sexist language is basic to all visions. Language is a tool of thought, a powerful method to create or exclude images.

WHAT IF universal networks of quality child care at health care institutions were established? This would have value for children, for parents and particularly, for all health practitioners' education. While use of child care opportunities by parents would be optional, the presence of these centers and the educational experience in them would not be optional for educators and students. Nurturance experience is central to health practice and a potentially humanizing experience for all practitioners of both sexes.

WHAT IF the gender-based division of labor in the health care system were eliminated? The basic division of labor in the life of humanity has been sex-linked. This has led to much (over)specialization, territorial "imperatives" and hierarchies, especially the valuing of tangible technical ("masculine") development over intangible, integrating social technologies ("feminine"). I foresee the specialist becoming recognized as the physical technician and the generalist-humanist emerging as the health leader. Some generalist-humanists will be nurses, some will be physicians, all will be educators in the most generic sense. Increasingly apparent is the reality that much of what makes people healthy or sick is other people and the quality of our interrelationships. Creative feminist-based social insights and technologies in the health care system itself may even become recognized as a major public health measure.

Desexigration of the health care system has enormous

implications for health care education, policy and research. The phenomenon of the male-female game; the still typical doctor-nurse game, has been noted by feminists.[47] Until health and other occupations are desexigrated, the work of the nurse in integrating, coordinating, quietly (if acknowledgedly) guiding total health care will be devalued. It must be valued not only quietly but publicly in law (practice acts, compensation regulations) and prestige. Instrumental and expressive dimensions in wholistic healing can only be more valued and strengthened by feminist insights – insights that are absent in patriarchal medical control.

Implications of Activism/Thought in Collaboration

An examination of significant societal changes reveals that many of the ideas now considered as truth originated in earlier, activist concerns that were often initially rejected by the professionals and "experts." What programs and proposals might we most progressively support, especially with public funds: those reflecting formalized but often secondary *thought,* or original and primary change agent *thinking,* or both? Much of the gut-level rhetoric of today's poor, the young, the racial minorities, aware women and/or homosexual people in demanding changes is becoming the cerebral process and academic preoccupation of tomorrow's scientists, scholars and academicians. These processes needn't be mutually exclusive.[48] Much of the thinking is prophetic, intuitive, and visionary. Activism based on visionary thinking has not yet been documented – it is not possible to document what has seldom, if ever, been tried.

Those who believe that we who are change agents, health activists, and prohetic scholars, are anti-science and too subjective are asked to consider the following. We are insisting that medicine and other would-be sciences be *more* scientific. A true scientific approach would eliminate the affluent white heterosexist, handicappist and androcentric prejudices and biases that are without any means of scientific support. Science means a body of facts and truths. Indeed, feminists are insistent on a "wholly new science of medicine and indeed health care: one that could integrate objective findings with the subjective experience of health or illness, that is, integrate the *curing* functions with the caring."[49] The new science would integrate and equally value the instrumental and expressive, the quantitative and qualitative, the cognitive and affective, indeed the "masculine" and "feminine" in values and people. Feminist values portend a significant imperative and a potential difference for individuals, health care, and indeed the body politic. *Assertive nurturance* is a concept I created to articulate the healing promises of gynandrous visions of people and our health care.

As a feminist wanting to translate private compassions into public health policy, I suspect that the foregoing few sample visions will soon appear myopic. In the human interest, I envision that these and other profound changes in health philosophies, practices, research, policies and practitioners will become, not a question of *if*, but questions of *when*, *where* and *how*. Women and men with changed feminist consciousness and confidence will create the difference – for the health of us all. I envision that the elimination of the artificial gender stereotyping and the consequent healing of the sex-based dimorphism will contribute significantly to the healing of the split of the world and its people.

NOTES

1. Rukeyser, Muriel: "Kathie Kollwitz" from *The Speed of Darkness* quoted in *The World Split Open.* (edited and introduced by Louise Bernikow) Random House, Inc., New York, NY, 1974.

2. Piercy, Marge: "A Work of Artiface" in *To Be Of Use.* illustrated by Lucia Varnarelli. Doubleday and Company, Garden City, NY, 1973.

3. Wildavsky, Aaron: "Doing Better and Feeling Worse: the Political Pathology of Health Policy." *Daedulus: Journal of the American Academy of Arts and Sciences.* Issue on Doing Better and Feeling Worse: Health in the United States. Winter 1977, Vol 106, No.1. p.105.

4. Braverman, Harry: *Labor and Monopoly Capital: the Degradation of Work in the Twentieth Century.* Monthly Review Press, 62 West 14th St., New York, NY 10011. 1974.

5. Seaman, Barbara: "Pelvic Anatomy: Four Proposals." *Social Policy.* September/October 1975, Vol. V Issue 5, pp.43-47. Also "Physician Heal Thy Self," *Proceedings of 1975 Conference on Women and Health.* c/o Box 192, West Somerville, MA 02114 ($2.00), pp. 25-27.

6. Arditti, Rita: "Male Contraception." *Science for the People.* (897 Main St., Cambridge, MA 02139) July 1976. 8:4, pp.12-15,35.

7. Burkans, D.M. and J.R. Wilson, "Is the Obstetrician-Gynecologist a Specialist or a Primary Physician to Women?" Paper presented to the American Association of Ostetricians and Gynecologists, September 4, 1975.

8. Marieskind, Helen: "Restructuring Ob-Gyn." Response to Barbara Seaman, *Social Policy,* September/October 1975. Vol.V Issue 5, pp. 48-49.

9. Pearson, Jack W: "The Obstetrician and Gynecologist, Primary Physician for Women." *Journal of the American Medical Association.* February 25, 1975. 231:8, 1975.

10. *Full Report on the Equal Rights Amendment.* Association of the Bar of the City of New York, 42 W. 44th Street, New York, NY 1975, pp.5,9.

11. Feminist Women's Health Center, 6411 Hollywood Blvd., Los Angeles, CA 90028. Publications include "How to Start Your Self-Help Clinic," ($2.50), and other resources written in Spanish and English.

12. *Women and Health.* SUNY College at Old Westbury, NY 11568.

13. Nurses NOW Task Force, Now Action Center, 425 13th Street, N.W., Washington DC 20004. Apparently national support for Nurses NOW evaporated about 1976. *Cassandra: Radical Feminist Nurses Network,* P.O. Box 341, Williamsville, NY 14221, was formed in 1982 and has begun to work toward similar goals.

14. "Nurses Rate Lawmakers – Identify Friends and Foes," *N-CAP News.* Summer, 1976, pp.1-4. Lobbying is not new for ANA; the overt, self-conscious political action identified by name is of recent origin. N-CAP, 1304 15th Street, N.W. Washington DC 20005.

15. NOW Legal Defense and Education Fund, 9 West 57 Street, New York, NY 10019; records of case of Association for Women in Science, et al, vs Richardson, Elliot, et al. (HEW Secretary); records of Dr. Julia Apter, spokesperson for Coalition of Professional Organizations, Rush Medical College, 1753 W. Congress Parkway, Chicago, IL 60612. Also see author's own records of change endeavors and the lawsuits and correspondence with Attorney Sylvia Roberts, Helen Hart Jones, and others (Schlesinger Library on the History of Women, Radcliffe).

16. *Taking Our Bodies Back.* Cambridge Documentary Films, a non-profit organization, P.O. Box 385, Cambridge, MA 02139.

17. Friedan, Betty: *The Feminine Mystique.* W.W. Norton Co., New York, NY 1963

18. Broverman, Inge, Donald Rosencrantz, Paul Vogel and Suzanne Vogel: "Sex Role Stereotypes and Clinical Judgements of Mental Health." *Journal of Consulting and Clinical Psychology.* February 1970. Vol. 34, Issue 1, p.1 -7.

19. Chesler, Phyllis: *Women and Madness.* Avon Books, New York, NY 1972.

20. Silver, Lani, Elyse Eisenberg, Katie Kain and Shelley Fern: "HEW OK's Federal Funds for Lobotomies." *Majority Report.* May 14-27, 1977. P. 5. 74 Grove St., New York, NY 10014.

21. Heide, Wilma Scott: "The Reality and the Challenge of the Double Standard in Mental Health." Symposium at Chatham College, Pittsburgh, PA, May 1969. Reprinted by KNOW, Inc., P.O. Box 86031, Pittsburgh, PA 15221.

22. Evansgardner, Jo Ann: "Notes on Founding." *Association for Women in Psychology.* 4393 N. MacGregor Way, Houston, TX 77004. 1969.

23. Downie, Mark and Tracy Johnston: "A Case of Corporate Malpractice." *Mother Jones: Magazine For The Rest of Us.* November 1976. 1:8, pp. 36-39, 46-50.

24. Brudney, Karen: "DES, The History." *Health Right.* Fall, 1975, Vol. 2, Issue 1, pp. 1,4.

25. *Health Right.* Women's Health Forum, 175 Fifth Avenue, NY, NY 10010. Vol 2, Issue 1, Fall 1975, p. 6.

26. "Critics Mount Attack on Agribusiness Firms." Community Nutrition Institution. Spring, 1976, 6:8, pp. 4-5. From Boston Women's Health Collective, Box 192, West Somerville, MA 02144.

27. Doerschuk, Bob: "Missionaries of Malnutrition: The MacDonald's Saga." Center For Science in The Public Interest. July 1976. 1755 Fifth Street, N.W., Washington, DC 20009.

28. Butterworth, Charles E. Jr., MD: "Physician-Induced Malnutrition." *National Nutrition Policy: Nutrition, Health and Development: A Working Paper.* Compiled by subpanel on Nutrition and Health Sciences for the Select Committee on Nutrition and Human Needs, U.S. Senate. Publication # 09956-62, Superintendent of Documents, U.S. Government Printing Office, Washington, DC 20402, May-June, 1974.

29. McGovern, George: "The Food Gap: Poverty and Malnutrition in the U.S." U.S. Senate Select Committee on Nutrition and Human Needs, 1970 Interim Report.

30. Boulding, Elise: *The Underside of History: A View of Women Through Time.* Westview Press, Boulder, CO, 1976.

31. Leghorn, Lisa and Mary Roodkowsky: *Who Really Starves? Women and World Hunger.* Friendship Press, 475 Riverside Drive, New York, NY, 1977.

32. Heide, Wilma Scott: "A Feminist's Perspectives on Manipulation of Woman." (Woman includes man and can be generic). Presented at symposium on The Genetic Manipulation of Man (sic), University of Wisconsin at Stevens Point, WI. November 8, 1973. Available from KNOW, INC., P.O. Box 86031, Pittsburgh, PA 15221

33. Arditti, Rita, Renate Duelli Klein and Shelley Minder (Eds.): *Test Tube Women.* Pandora Press, 9 Park St., Boston, MA 02108, 1984. See also Gena Corea: *The Mother Machine.* Harper and Row, 1985.

34. My notes on the NOW representatives meeting with the EEOC.

35. Heide, Wilma Scott: "Racial Justice and Feminism; Common Causes in the Human Interest." Prepared for Wellesley College while a guest in residence. Available from Harambee House, Wellesley College, Wellesley, MA 02181.

36. Stellman, Jeanne and Susan Daum: *Work Is Dangerous To Your Health: A Handbook of Health Hazards In The Workplace And What You Can Do About Them.* Random House, New York, NY. 1971 and 1973. Also book by Jeanne Stellman: *Women's Work, Women's Health: Myths And Realities.* Pantheon Books, NY, 1977.

37. "...To Form A More Perfect Union: Justice for American Women." Report of the National Commission on the Observance of International Women's Year, The Women's Bureau, U.S. Department of Labor, Washington, DC, 1976.

38. Kapur, Promilla: "Myth or Reality: Equal Rights." *World Health.* WHO January 1975, pp. 8-11. Avenue Appia, 1211, Geneva 27, Switzerland, $.70/copy.

39. Hosken, Fran P: *The Hosken Report: Genital And Sexual Mutilation of Females.* Available from W.I.News, 187 Grant Street, Lexington, MA 02173. 1979, $12.00 prepaid.

40. Russell, Diana and Nicole Van Ven: "Crimes Perpetrated by the Medical Profession." *The Proceedings of The International Tribunal On Crimes Against Women.* 1976. Les Femmes Publishing, 231 Adrian Road, Millbrae, CA 84030. $ 5.95.

41. International Feminist Planning Conference convened by NOW, National Organization for Women, Inc., Summary book edited by Ernesta P. Ballard and Jean Byrne. NOW, 425 13th St. NW, Washington, DC 20004. $4.00.

42. Heide, Wilma Scott: "Feminism for Healthy Social Work." Commencement Address, Smith College School of Social Work. August 20, 1975. Taped and transcribed in *Smith College School Of Social Work Journal.* Winter 1976. 3:1. pp. 1-4.

43. Rossi, Alice: "A Biosocial Perspective on Parenting." *Daedulus: Journal of The American Academy of Arts And Sciences.* Issue on the Family. Spring 1977. 106:2, pp. 1-31.

44. Heide, Wilma Scott: "Towards a Feminist School of Medicine." A proposal prepared for the Special Task Force on Women and Health and presented to the Society of Health and Human Values, Philadelphia, PA. January 1971.

45. Howell, Mary: "A Women's Health School?" *Social Policy.* September-October 1975. Vol. V, Issue 5, pp. 50-53.

46. Miller, Jean Baker: *Toward A New Psychology of Women.* Beacon Press, Boston. 1976.

47. Heide, Wilma Scott: "Nursing and Women's Liberation: A Parallel." *American Journal of Nursing.* May 1973. 73:5, pp. 824-827.

48. Heide, Wilma Scott: "Some Egalitarian* Alternatives to Androcentric Science." Presented at the American Psychological Convention Symposium: What Can the Behavioral Sciences Do to Modify the World so that Women Who Want to Participate Meaningfully Are not Regarded as and are Not, in Fact, Deviant? September 3, 1969. *Egalitarian means equality of all men, thus a more appropriate word I would now use is feminist.

49. Marieskind, Helen and Barbara Ehrenreich: "Toward Socialist Medicine: The Women's Health Movement." *Social Policy.* September-October 1975. Vol. V, Issue 5, pp. 41-43.

CHAPTER THREE

SCHOLARSHIP:
ACTION IN THE HUMAN INTEREST

Scholarship is a kind of action; informed action requires scholarship. Whether in higher education, health care or elsewhere, scholarship and other forms of activism are and need to be mutually supportive, not mutually exclusive within individuals and organizations. The best research is imbedded in effective social action and vice versa. Effective social action requires sound research, which in turn is sound in part precisely because it is related to action. Formulating knowledge is action. Activists and scholars can inform each other and integrate their endeavors in covenants with truth.

Both activists and scholars can be on the frontiers of new horizons; the boundaries of both are hardly known. It is not that activists/scholars have been too bold. Indeed, we have yet to be audacious enough to move from re-search to future-search. Future-search poses different questions, hypothesizes *WHAT IF* possibilities, questions conclusions accepted as "givens," and challenges the premises and prisms of conventional scholarship and its interrelationships to the human interest.

Scholarship examines and shapes human affairs, as does activism. All activism and scholarship arise from political intent and have political implications. The allegation that feminist scholarship is biased is false. Feminist scholarship moves the center of gravity from men-only to women *and* men, to men *and* women. Bias and its onus rests clearly with androcentric scholarship. The feminist balancing shift cannot, in truth, be designated as biased, but rather as a perspective that eliminates bias.

A Feminist Perspective on Scholarship

The current international feminist movement will ultimately be recognized as the most profound phenomenon of this century in its positive potential for radical changes in the quality of life. Interestingly, most scholars did not predict this. Those who did were involved with the feminist movement or were potential activists as well.

The immense potential for radical change arising from feminism rests on the fact that feminism is unbiased. Scholars, researchers and academicians cannot continue to countenance the stated or implied allegation that to be feminist is to be biased. It is the remarkable *contrast* of feminism with patriarchal bias that inaccurately places the onus of bias on feminism, rather than on androcentric sexism where it belongs. A philosophy that envisions elimination of human supremacy based on sex, race, income, religion, age, ethnicity and/or sexual preference is unbiased precisely because it rejects extant prejudices. Androcentric scholarship is consequent to and causative of supremacy claims of and for classes of people. Sexism is merely normal but not natural. Feminism is not yet normal though it is very natural. In a healthy society and world, that which is natural would be also normal.

Related to the issue of bias is the value assignment of what is "important." There are those who see the goals and objectives of the women's movement as important but separate and unrelated to the "real issues" of this nation and world. Actually, issues that are called the "real issues" are derivative of and indivisible from both the state of underdevelopment of many women worldwide and the unrecognized development of many women. In addition, feminists are painfully aware of the underdevelopment of many men in significant areas and men's inflated allegations of development without substantive supportive evidence. The fragile male ego itself is a real issue of gigantic proportions. The perspective that suggests the needs of women are unrelated to the allegedly larger economic and political considerations as some scholars imply or state, simply fails to acknowledge the oppression of women in perpetuating existing economic and political conditions. Sexism determines the basic character of what are *called* the larger economic and political issues. Feminist perspectives are a *sine qua non* for understanding the human condition and for *all* identification and solving of human problems. Feminism is not a panacea but it is a *bona fide occupational qualification* for valid and relevant scholarship.

Feminist scholarship employs imagination; it is consciously value-oriented in contrast to the predominantly non-conscious value-orientation of traditional scholarship. Feminist scholarship is informed by other actions of the past, present and possible future. Action informs the scholar of that precious experiential knowledge that comes only from testing and stretching what is possible.

Feminist scholarship is a transdisciplinary approach. It is disciplined by eschewing:

- fragmentation of knowledge that can weaken thought;
- specialization that avoids connections to wholeness;
- technical "reasoning" that quantifies more and more about less and less so that qualitative processes of life seem nonexistent because they can't be measured;
- theorizing and generalizing phenomena without concrete applications;
- distancing of oneself from real people so much as to be irrelevant to life or lives.

Feminists insist on unshackling those focused orders of academia which arbitrarily compartmentalize and limit grander visions of human potential.

Future Search

Feminist scholarship is more accurately called future-search than re-search, which is focused on the past. Feminists are futurists and prophets as are other change agents; the cognitive and affective minority, who have visions of humanity and the affairs of the world that transcend contemporary acceptable views. Re-search is looking backward, with a focus on perpetuating the status quo. The following sections present ideas for scholarship that focus on the future based on feminist values.

On Leadership

Are men because they are men and socialized normally (not necessarily naturally), qualified for public leadership? In addressing this question I refer to those aspects of male socialization that encourage and reward power *for* oneself and power *over* others and that emphasize control *over* others to avoid control *by* others. Further, male socialization normally (not naturally) emphasizes self interest and considers secondarily, others' interests. In contrast, female socialization normally (not naturally) emphasizes others' interests and secondarily, self interest.

Even woman's "self interest" focuses heavily on behaviors designed to attract and/or please men unless and until feminist consciousness develops. Yet, the nurturance of self and others and the courage to risk are both leadership qualities. Thus, both normal male and normal female socialization disqualifies an individual for leadership and power. Neither of the traditional socialization processes equips an individual to represent the interests of self and others combined. Scholarship that perpetuates the "normal" processes of socialization is likewise disqualified.

Even more fundamental would be scholarship that creates developmental gynandry of positive "feminine" and "masculine" strengths as a basis for evaluating leadership criteria for access to power. The proclivity to use power to control others would be a negative evaluation of existing leadership, resulting in a conclusion of disqualification. Surely, the question for scholars is not whether women are qualified for leadership and power, but rather, are men?

Another reconceptualization of leadership qualification would be the demonstrated commitment to indivisible human rights as a bona fide occupational qualification (BFOQ) for eligibility to be even considered for elective or appointive public office, for publicly funded (in whole or part) college and university positions. Such a BFOQ is infinitely more valid and relevant than age, citizenship, sex, race, income, and/or sexual preference factors that still exist in selection processes.

Scholars of future search and vision might well rethink and reformulate the potential of serving the human interest with imaginative evaluations of leadership and power derived from feminist ethics. It should be no more difficult to make operational the qualifications suggested than, for example, assessing intelligence, communication skills, integrity or administrative abilities in evaluating leadership.

Academic Tenure

Do academic tenure criteria reflect proportionately the life experiences, insights and values of those who are not male, not white and/or not affluent? If not, the criteria for tenure decisions are not a valid basis for granting virtual lifetime job security for education in the human interest. Guaranteed lifetime tenure *itself* may inhibit change in an ostensibly democratic society where change is the only constant. Academic freedom in publicly supported institutions must not include the license to teach or use materials that perpetuate human wrongs such as racism or sexism that are contrary to civil rights, legal and ethical imperatives. If tenure is a valid means of assuring academic freedom (its original purpose), tenure criteria and decisions should be re-examined periodically by the academic community. Responsible scholar/activists must resolve the value conflicts within their own community, with a shift to feminist values.

Patriarchy, Militarism and Demilitarism

Are there causes and effects as well as positive relationships between variations of patriarchy (with consequent sexism and sex-role polarization) and militarism of a nation, and conversely, between feminism and demilitarism? Would systematic cross-cultural feminist analyses of these phenomena relate to humane social structures and systems?

To move from militarism to demilitarism to positively peaceful values and behaviors means not only re-searching, but future searching the positive correlations *and* the cause and effect relationships between:

- nurturance and peace in private and public policies,
- "feminine" strengths and diminished dominance politics, and
- changes in casts of characters and scripts in public policy areas.

In 1973 I spoke with Alva Myrdal of Sweden, internationally known peace and disarmament scholar/writer who had not been planning to examine machismo factors in conceptualizing and studying conditions and climates for disarmament and peace. Because this person is often characterized as a feminist, I was especially surprised to realize the low levels of consciousness on this, but heartened to see the person taking notes on ideas, approaches, and resources.

Sweden is virtually surrounded by countries whose records include military aggression and adventurism. Yet, Sweden has not been involved in war for over a century. While I think Sweden's socialist policies play an important role, Sweden's additional public policies and practices that are consistent with feminist values are crucial. A feminist scholar might ask: What are the positive correlations between feminist policies and practices and a nation's non-military behavior? Do feminist policies result in unaggressive philosophies and economic expenditures for social needs?

Sexuality: Whose Norms?

Another rich area for future-search is sexuality. A feminist approach to the issue of sexuality would pose questions radically – fundamentally – differently than those of traditional scholarship. Feminist scholarship would examine the phenomena that create an apparent majority of women being primarily (apparently) heterosexual in a patriarchal society such as the United States. Is this pathological in a culture that institutionalizes misogyny, some of it subtly? Granted, misogyny itself and women's financial insecurity discourages lesbianism. However, given the extent of violence against women in a misogynistic society, more homosexuality among women would be expected as the norm. Indeed, except for the bedroom and related phenomena, both men and women are more homosocial or monosocial than heterosocial. Future-search that poses bisexuality or lesbianism as the norms, and exclusive heterosexuality (especially by women) as deviance, would radicalize the approaches of scholarship on sexuality. Deviance would be interpreted as any behavior that is contrary to the political best interests of women. What is posed here is the elimination of heterosexist bias in research in order to learn what *is* natural.

Interrelationships of Sexism and Racism

One crucial area where scholars of the future could make a profound difference is in rethinking concepts about the anti-humanisms of racism and sexism, their uniqueness and interrelationships.

In 1957, I visited Little Rock, Arkansas, as a sociologist-journalist to interview the white women shown on TV along with white men who were adamantly opposed to school desegregation. There was no question about the virulent racism of the angry whites. Although a civil rights activist, I was there not to judge but to learn how these women felt about their lives. My interviewing was nondirective.

One woman's question was typical and particularly revealing: "If we, as women, can stay in our places as women, why can't the nigras [sic] stay in their places?" The women I interviewed realized even as they talked that they perceived it was safer to *oppose* change vis-à-vis the races than to *advocate* changes in their own status and roles as women, and in relations to and with men. Challenging their own status as women was a revelation and a possibility even more unsettling and unthinkable to them than racial integration of schools.

Almost two decades later in Boston we again witnessed white women in the leadership of anti-integration and anti-busing. The organization Restore Our Alienated Rights (ROAR) was actively opposed to de-segregation. What is revealed in the choice of the phrase "alienated rights," is the white women's fear that they might lose that one area of power where they have had or wanted some say, ie, in the schooling of their children. I submit that some displaced feelings and actions about power and self-empowerment alleviates some of the constraints of sexism for women (in this case, white) and exacerbates racism. The fact that most of those in Boston who opposed school racial desegregation also opposed the Equal Rights Amendment (ERA) and other human rights extensions supports this conjecture.

Laws and Their Enforcement

Police work is 90% social work, according to Police Foundation studies, yet much of police training is in use of hardware, firearms and instrumentalized containment of victims of institutionalized injustices. Future-search scholars focused on feminist values in the human interest would do well to explore occupational requirements for the situations police encounter. If existing studies and considered observations about the social work component of police work are indeed validated, scholars could collaborate with activists and dramatists to educate police for the jobs that they are called upon to do, and to educate the public about the services police could provide.

Another reconceptualization of police work is inclusion of enforcement of civil rights laws related to employment, education, housing, public accommodations, as well as enforcement of laws on public order and safety. Police workers often selectively enforce laws and differentially apply those they do enforce by race, sex and income level. This does not mean the end of civil rights enforcement agencies, but augmentation of their work by sensitizing police to the relevance of operative, indivisible civil rights.

The lack of seriousness with which the body politic takes civil rights, as reflected in differential punishments for violation of these laws and anti-burglary felonies is appalling. For example, an employer can violate an equal employment opportunity law that denies a qualified employee the potential to earn money in the hundreds or thousands of dollars, yet receive less (if any) punishment than the individual who steals one hundred dollars from that employer. The significant difference is not only the amount of money involved but the differential power. The 1964 Civil Rights Law provides a greater penalty for violation of the confidentiality protection of the alleged violator than the penalty to the employer for proven violation(s) of Title VII (which forbids discrimination in employment on grounds of race, religion, nationality, color or sex). Employers charged with violations of civil rights laws are protected from public exposure by the confidentiality provision in the law until guilt is established. Individuals who have allegedly burglarized can have their names publicized, suffer indignities, denial of freedom and arrest.

What I'm suggesting is that scholars use different (including feminist) perspectives on these and other areas of justice and injustice, and examine the possibility that affluent white patriarchal law represents an obstruction of justice.

Feasibility/Simulation Projects

The following are some suggested feasibility and/or simulation projects that scholars could conduct that would contribute to possibilities for change in the human interest. WHAT IF possibilities provide visions of what is possible. Details of the design of the work can be created by those intrigued enough to explore the potential.

WHAT IF women and girls did not feel constrained to and did not, in fact, obey any laws that refer only to: he, his, him, man or men? These are male-only words and are not generic for both sexes. Until the language is changed, and until the U.S. Constitutional Equal Rights Amendment (ERA) is ratified and implemented and a state ERA is implemented, such non-compliance on exclusionary grounds would be a valuable educational experience. The participants would necessarily include citizens, legislators and lawyers. Scholars, researchers and activists who design such experimental projects could communicate the results to reach a far wider audience.

WHAT IF compulsory attendance until age 16 in schools that still blatantly or subtlely teach girls to be subservient, subordinate and/or submissive were considered violations of the XIII Amendment to the U.S. Constitution, which prohibits involuntary servitude? The litigation process of this issue could make an edifying scholarly research project. It could strengthen or hasten enforcement of Title IX of the 1972 Education Amendments. Title IX prohibits discrimination based on sex in schools that receive any public federal money – all do. It could also serve as public education about the way girls learn about their presumed "inferiority" to males and how boys learn the mythologies of their presumed "superiority" to females.

WHAT IF population scholars/researchers were committed to population choices rather than population control? Experimental and non-experimental groups from indigenous populations in the United States and elsewhere could be studied to determine the effects of feminist programs, compared to several other programs offering choices about parenthood. The feminist approach would not be either anti-natalist or pro-natalist, but would explore with people the parental options for adults of both sexes.

I am constantly and alternatively mystified and amused at the little or no attention that the United States and most other western population analysts appear to give to the changed consciousness of women and men that has resulted from the women's movement. Population control is antithetical to feminist ethics of self-choice and so feminism's rebirth has provided a climate of choice. A diminution of birth rates has occurred during the same time period (1966-1976). It would be instructive to know if a direct relationship between choice and reduced birth rates could be demonstrated.

WHAT IF scholars focused on a feminist approach in the law? Law, as conceptualized and practiced in the United States relies on precedent and tradition. It has thus been backward, not forward-looking. Precedent and tradition repeatedly inform us that United States law is and has been that of the affluent, heterosexual, white and patriarchal male. Thus, the law is not necessarily in the human interest of the some 90% of the population who are not affluent, not white, not heterosexual, and/or not male.

Most law is adversarial in concept and practice, reflecting androcentric values as in Smith *versus* Jones. A feminist characterization and approach would be in the interests of justice for Smith *and* Jones. Adversarial law assumes a "winner" and a "loser," yet disputes over behavior are frequently not so clear cut about what is just and unjust. Anne Strick observed that the adversarial system requires everyone who uses the law to settle differences to behave as fighting enemies, and the harder the enemies fight the better. The false assumption is that truth will be revealed out of this battle; this has been called "the fighting theory of justice," and underlies both the conceptual framework and the practice of law. Rather than revealing what is known, each side discloses only partial truths – each intent on discovery and avoiding discovery of hidden truths.[1]

The law is really a codification of positively and negatively sanctioned behavior and not necessarily resulting in "justice." Feminist law, committed to sexual, racial and economic justice, could make a profound difference in the nature and quality of social institutions. Demographic representation in the law by sex, race and income level would radically change the cast of characters and the script. Feminist approaches to the law would be non-adversarial in concept and process. What is proposed here is future-search on and creation of such phenomena.

WHAT IF feminist scholars with economic experience identified sources of funds for feminist change and publicized this widely within the women's movement? As of 1980, foundations gave less than one fifth of one percent of their funds for feminist projects, even by the most generous definitions. Currently feminist organizations and groups committed to change have relatively limited knowledge of sources of money and methods to obtain these funds. The delineation of how feminism addresses changes that *are* supported by monied groups could be developed. Several important areas already receive funding, such as child welfare. Areas not funded, but which need to be, include: reduction of violence, conditions for peace, quality of life, healthy family structures, political maturity, reduction of or (better) the elimination of poverty (among others). These areas require feminist perspectives, analyses and approaches in order to achieve even their own stated goals, let alone more radical and fundamental change.

In truth, I'm not particularly sanguine about the early educability of those who hold the purse strings of groups that perpetuate sexism and the resultant human problems attributed to other origins. The source and the values of those who control the main sources of money in our society are often intimately connected to the causes of social problems. Nonetheless, the monied and their agents must be presumed to be educable. While liberal feminism, pseudo-feminism and non-feminism are more easily funded than more radical projects, the former are supported precisely for the reasons that they promise (threaten?) little or no significant changes. The more radical feminists, whose pressures in the early 1970's changed the climate of awareness so that some financial support is now possible, have been ignored, disclaimed, and de-energized or diminished in resources.

The problem of funding is a moral question and a question of integrity for both the money dispensers and scholars/academicians. If any reader thinks I'm suggesting the responsibility and opportunity for scholars/researchers to develop funding and support, and share this in collaboration with more overtly direct-action people, s/he is 100% correct. The risks (being honest about feminist perspectives) and rewards must be shared by scholars/activists in solidarity. Women in particular, and society in general, can simply not afford more evidence of obvious sexism without implemented methods/actions to eliminate the branch, trunk and roots of sexism in funding. If the roots of feminist change are not nourished, the derivative branches and leaves cannot survive.

WHAT IF scholars with feminist insights studied institutions like the Center for the Study of Democratic Institutions, the World Future Society and the World Bank?

The employment pattern of the Center for the Study of Democratic Institutions (CSDI) do not even reach current token standards. The white patriarchal orientation of the CSDI is something to behold. Such a center cannot truly conceptualize or study democracy. For nearly three years (1971-1974) NOW recommended, corresponded about, wrote proposals for the Center addressing the issues raised by the women's movement and the potential the women's movement portended in the context of true democratic institutions.

In 1974, the Center co-sponsored (with the University of California at Santa Barbara) a two-day symposium on "Social and Political Change: The Role of Women" which resulted in a 1976 book, *Women in the World, A Comparative Study.*[2] Only academic scholars (*not* including those who were also the NOW leaders proposing Center involvement) were invited. Further, only the safe (albeit vital and important) issues of global changes were discussed. The book which reported the discussions included less than six pages out of 411, on "Political Change for [not by] the American Women." Even that is a summary of what *has been*, rather than what *could be*. Except for parts of the introductory "Patriarchal Heritage," the discussions in this publication concerned countries a safe distance from the United States (the Center's home) and the viable women's movement in the United States. One can only question the Center's validity, their democratic pretenses, and lack of courage to confront the present – let alone the future.

The name of the World Future Society (WFS) is a misnomer considering its predominantly American membership and its leaderships' ignorance about the present, never mind the future. Neither the CSDI nor the WFS would matter much, except that some people in leadership roles take these groups seriously as having expertise about democracy and the future.

The Society's 1971 and 1975 Assemblies had, as traditionally, only establishment white men addressing "The Future of Mankind" (sic), although months were spent in attempts to change these orientations. While there are WFS members who are genuinely concerned about creating alternative humane futures, many influential members are not. For example, Herman Kahn was an architect of Vietnam "pacification" of indigent populations; the U.S. Senate consults Kahn and other members of the Society on technology assessment.

As a feminist activist/scholar, I organized with others an alternative conference at the WFS 1975 Assembly in rejection of the Society's white, patriarchal, technocratic, linear orientations. The WFS president threatened me with arrest though nothing illegal occurred. Armed security, ordered by the president, followed me everywhere; I even became "friends" with them. Alvin Toffler, author of *Future Shock* and *The Third Wave*, often consulted about the future by policy makers, felt obliged to publicly support the alternative conference.

Before embarking on an analysis of the money-gathering, money-dispensing World Bank, some results of existing feminist scholarship might be instructive:

- the World Bank's billions of dollars comes from the public, much of it from the United States;
- the president of the Bank was Robert McNamara, former Vietnam fiasco "Defense Secretary" and before that, President of Ford Motors;
- after feminist pressure in 1974 and 1975, the World Bank contracted for a study of its employment practices. The Bank refused to release or share the study results. Even though public money paid for the study, the details of the study were not available to the public.
- McNamara stated that he believes that poverty and overpopulation are the world's most serious problems and should be the World Bank's top priorities;
- however, the top executive, policy-making staff are *all male*. Yet women are the most impoverished in every country in the world, and women's lack of participation in changing women's status and roles is central to women's procreational underemployment; ie, women's economic viability is key to reduced births and elimination of poverty.
- McNamara did not realize the World Bank, as constituted, is part of the problem, not part of the solution of poverty and population pressures. Indeed, he accepts humanitarianism awards in spite of these profound caveats.
- In 1976, a black woman was appointed to the World Bank staff. Questions about "minorities"[3] and women became her responsibility while the male top decision-makers continued to make decisions for and about women's lives. The introduction of any *one* person, however talented, cannot change the World Bank's essential patriarchy.

Feminist scholarship is needed to evaluate the goals, the ethos, the staff composition, the results and the influence of all these institutions and organizations, as well as similar ones. The results of such studies need to be widely communicated in professional journals and in the public media. Activists have done the preliminary scholarship and could be key consultants for those who wish to pursue significant scholarship beyond esoteric studies that merely augment one's publications vita.

I wonder what serious scholarship might reveal about the correlations between unsolved problems and limited insights of traditional scholars who serve to "inform" would-be leaders and policy makers. Is traditional scholarship one dimension which disqualifies one to conceptualize social problems? Daniel Patrick Moynihan's limitation of insights vis-à-vis black families and Eli Ginsberg's deficiencies vis-à-vis women are two of many cases in point. Moynihan considered matriarchy to be pathological but patriarchy to be ideal and healthy. Ginsberg, while chair of a federal manpower (sic) commission, recommended that a woman be denied employment if her husband was employed but not that a man be denied employment if his wife was employed.

WHAT IF scholars examined the manipulation of governmental agencies by giant corporations? Using blatant double standards, the corporations pick and choose which laws to obey, which to resist or ignore. A case in point is "Pa" Bell – American Telephone & Telegraph Co. (AT&T) – America's largest civilian employer. AT&T is also among the top six Pentagon contractors. When asked by Dr. Sally Hacker about their heavy military involvement, former Board Chairone Romnes stated that AT&T responds to the country's needs "as defined by responsible agencies of government." Yet, the EEOC, a responsible agency of government, found that "Pa" Bell tried massive resistance by initially going to court rather than responding legally and affirmatively to the country's equal employment opportunity policies and needs.[4] The EEOC had 2,700 pages of documentation of AT&T's violations of the Employment Title VII of the 1964 Civil Rights Law and the 1972 Equal Employment Opportunity Law.

WHAT IF scholars studied the social impact of proposed legislation not only on women but by women? Currently, activists without support funding are doing most of this type of legislative research work and their limited resources produce a focus on impact of legislation on women. Future-search by activists/scholars could help move society from perpetuating images of women as people acted-upon to realities of women as pro-active, and thus acting on women's lives and on public policies in public roles.

WHAT IF scholars did critical incident studies of sexism and televised the results on commercial networks as documentaries, including feminist alternatives as corrective programs?

The critical incident technique is a method to identify incidents where the behavioral objective is known. The situation is observed to identify which behavior is critical in achieving the objective and which behavior is ineffective. An incident is critical when the specific behavior reflects and contributes to the objective, or conversely, is ineffective when the behavior does not reflect/contribute to the known objective. Assume the known objective is non-sexist behavior. A few incidents may be isolated behaviors, not necessarily reflective of institutional practice. Hundreds of incidents of behaviors in representative areas of human interaction would provide a picture of patterns and practices, however non-conscious. This is not behavioral modification of the powerless by the powerful. It is behavioral elucidation to promote understanding.

Numerous incidents are rich in human drama. Especially rich are the apparently commonplace, taken-for-granted behaviors that can be teased out to be dramatized (not exaggerated) and thus made visibly obvious. Daily incidents create the climate of where and how people work, study, communicate and live. Dramatization of these daily incidents presented through the media of television could bring to public consciousness an understanding of how these incidents perpetuate a sexist society.

Television stations are licensed in the public interest; 95% of homes have TV. Most people's lives are microcosms, where connections to macrocosmic public issues may be more real than apparent. The collaborations of scholars, activists and dramatists, could dynamically document both sexism and feminist alternatives. Television stations and networks have both the responsibility and the opportunity to confront sexism. So do scholars/activists.

WHAT IF feminist future-searchers created feminist institutes and institutions?

Over several decades, I've visited campuses of "higher" learning, as a short-term (2-7 days) feminist-in-residence (sometimes with other euphemistic titles) sponsored jointly by one or several nearby institutions. Wherever this has occurred feminist scholars/academicians on and off campus collaborated to make it happen. In many of those visits, the idea of creating feminist institutes and institutions arises from activists. A few days of overt feminism, in collaboration with academicians, can be countenanced, even welcomed by the patriarchal system because it "takes the steam" out of a real or potential pressure cooker. It does not a feminist institution make. Nor does a residency happen unless those with scholarly and academic, as well as feminist credentials, see and act on what feminism portends for academia, scholarship and virtually everything else. The residency is a interim phenomenon of value to be extended in numbers and length.

In a sense, a women's university is already in formation in the increasingly serious and purposeful writings of women, women's studies programs, feminist presses, formal and informal communications networks, bookstores, infiltration of the library system and associations, multi-media creations, women's centers, professional and academic caucuses, countless conferences and much more learner-initiated re-socialization. This university has no buildings and no boundaries. Throughout this work, there is an intense commitment to the quality of human life rather than individual achievement of "success."

Feminist institutions could seek geographic locations for communications flow and meeting space, or may eschew that, but would somehow organize to support the visions and the visionaries of thought and action for change. A few scholars ensconsed in academia and the world of research are conjoined with activists. However, those individuals who are most likely to be direct action-oriented are those in touch with, if not among, those who are poor, who are minority members, who work in the lowest-paid occupations. Beginning support for feminist projects risks the tyrannies of tokenism and elitism if confined to the multi-degreed and recognized scholars. The creation of feminist institutions will rest on collaboration between scholars and those who are in the forefront of transcending conventional "wisdoms." The vision of feminist institutions opens a possibility to create cross-fertilization of thought, action and change, empowering and nurturing us all to search for and create a future worth the quest.

WHAT IF we studied men qua men, not as generic for human beings but as a sex in the context of gender studies. To eliminate historic androcentric sex-identified bias, feminist women would need to be the principal investigators to assure scientific objectivity – as much as humanly possible.

WHAT IF we studied those who use the phrase "post-feminism." We would scrutinize symptoms of wishful thinking; evidence of superficial understandings of social-political movements; positive fealty to androcentricity; t.t.p. (terminal testosterone poisoning) by sex or uncritical association.

Implications of Scholarship/Activism in Collaboration

Feminist consciousness of scholars and academicians both *as –* *and* in collaboration *with* – activists has far-reaching implications and applications. Consciousness (and its raising) is an educational means of creating awareness of new-found and rediscovered truths, as well as simply reviewing information with fresh perspectives. Scholars, academicians and activists seek to create, discover and/or share knowledge. Knowing requires critical reflection upon given and created truths. Knowledge is most fertile, (that is – least sterile) when joined with action.

Jean Baker Miller in her visionary book, *Toward A New Psychology of Women* [5] [actually, of women, men and society], reminds us that insight develops only *after* one begins to change something. As a behavioral scientist, a scholar and an activist, I can attest to the profound contributions that change activism had in sharpening my perceptions. The action brought to light realization of how things really are and how to create societal values that could be in the human interest. Other scholars and academicians who were persuaded to participate in direct actions (often for the first time), inform me that they can never again distance themselves in abstractions and alleged objectivity. The dichotomy between action and abstraction is androcentric, artificial and ultimately dysfunctional.

Scholars who attempt to discredit and to invalidate the synergy and synthesis of activism and scholarship do so at the risk of their own work being and becoming esoteric, and eminently forgettable, however "valid" in the eyes of status quo androcentrics. Leffler and others have written how academic feminists "rarely research new topics or develop new ideas," but rather "trail in the movement's wake (without acknowledging movement inspiration or genesis of issue development)."[6,p.12-13] However understandable it is to appreciate the career risks of identifying with the movement, eschewing the general primacy of activists in movements is neither acceptable nor affordable.

Feminism has yet to be understood and taken seriously enough by the usual contemporary commentators and chroniclers to know whose and what work will endure and make a difference. In my view, some who are doing the most profound and vital work have no "press agents" and are not well known inside, let alone outside, the movement. The research centers, whose hands are out for monetary benefits, seldom include or even consult with those whose necks were/are out to confront issues, raise consciousness, unequivocally press without compromise so that even the monied establishment is at least giving a token response.

All the initially unpopular causes that ultimately change the course of human history had origins in the streets, in sweatshops, in student dorms, in women's coffee klatches; not in legislatures, oval offices, corporate board rooms or research sanctuaries. The actions that made the difference arose out of existential experience of human need, not dispassionate discourses and intellectual gymnastics.

Who/what sustains and nurtures change activists so that we can avoid marginal existence or premature death, but instead positively nourish the life of our most profound thoughts and engage in audacious actions? For the inspired to survive and thrive, women's well-learned and valuable nurturance must address and solve this problem. Feminism critiques what is and creates alternatives to patriarchy in thought, actions and institutions. This task is not for sunshine matriots, careerists, fair-weather faddists or ladylike leeches. Passion is necessary to empower courage, prophetic vision, intellectual originality, psychic energy and commitment to create and sustain change movements.

The list of possibilities I've presented is in no way exhaustive, but it is a call to scholars and academicians to live, as well as future-search the ideas, to embrace feminism in order to heal the alienations of patriarchy.

NOTES

1. Strick, Ann: "What's Wrong With the Adversary System: Paranoia, Hatred and Suspicion." *The Washington Monthly.* January, 1977. pp. 19-28. Also see her book *Injustice For All,* G.P. Putnam's and Sons, 1977.

2. Iglitzen, Lynne B. and Ruth Ross (Eds.): *Women in the World: A Comparative Study.* Studies in Comparative Politics Series. Ohio Books, 2040 Almeda Padre Serra, Santa Barbara, Ca 93103, 1976.

3. "minorities" is in quotes here because people of color are two-thirds of the world's population and women are over one-half. That makes white males less than one-sixth of the world's adult population.

4. Hacker, Sally and Burt Hacker: unpublished letter to the editor of *Ms. Magazine,* November 30, 1973. At the time this letter was written Sally Hacker was the NOW Coordinator for studies of AT&T. Dr. Hacker did post-doctoral study on AT&T while at M.I.T. in 1977-1978 and shared her findings from that study with me.

5. Miller, Jean Baker: *Toward a New Psychology of Women.* Beacon Press, Boston. 1976.

6. Leffler, A., D. Gillespie, and E. Ratner: "Academic Feminists and the Women's Movement." *Ain't I A Woman?* Vol. 4, No. 1. 1973.

CHAPTER FOUR

ECONOMICS: BREASTIMONY ON H.R. 9030

"WELFARE REFORM"

The quest for our humanity via education, healthy health care and activist scholarship may be luxuries for those struggling to survive, though surely the quality of the former will influence the character and cast of characters of the latter. In 1977 and 1979, the Carter-Mondale Administration proposed Welfare Reform (sic). The legislation, H.R. 9030, tells a lot about how and if those in political leadership positions understand poverty, countenance it, and address and listen to its victims.

In November 1977 I provided written Breastimony to the Welfare Reform Subcommittee of the Committees on Agriculture, Education and Labor, and Ways and Means in the U.S. House of Representatives. The term used in the original document, as in all similar instances, was 'testimony'. The origin of the word 'testimony' is described in the Women's Encyclopedia of Myths and Secrets *as follows:*

> Patriarchal Semites worshipped their own genitals, and swore binding oaths by placing a hand on each other's private parts, a habit still common among the Arabs. Words like testament, testify, and testimony still *attest* to the oaths sworn on the testicles.[1,p.793-794]

Thus, 'testimony' is appropriate for males only and is not generic for all people. I use the word 'Breastimony' now to emphasize the shift that a woman-identified perspective creates in relation to these issues.

The words 'Breastify' and 'Breastimony' were created in 1980 when some of us in the greater Boston area were working as Feminist Women for Peace preparing to share our insights on the then-proposed National Peace Academy (finally accepted as the National Peace Institute in 1984).

This chapter and the next contain the edited version of my Breastimony. Notes at the end of each chapter provide updated information regarding some of the points made at the time of the Breastimony. Regretfully, real progress is yet to be seen in many of these areas and the Breastimony remains relevant today. This chapter contains the portion of my Breastimony that analyzes the legislative proposals and recommends improvements in or total reconstruction of the proposed legislation. The next chapter contains future-search ideas for real wel-fare re-form.

Clearly, the Administration and Congress needed feminist education to overcome their poverty of imagination for true re-forming of welfare programs. But this bill, however inadequate, was the best I had seen proposed by the Federal government in the past 30 years. Even so, H.R. 9030 would have been a travesty of justice. H.R. 9030 was not passed. No legislation of any scope, let alone comparable scope vis-à-vis welfare has been proposed since. In fact, what has happened is a retreat by Reagan and his white male-oriented club from even the moderate proposals of H.R. 9030. Instead, various forms of punitive work-fare have been proposed or instituted in some states and localities. Well-fare has been reserved for the special interest of the military folks and the industries and businesses which supply them.

This legislation and the Carter-Mondale Administration Plan were generally referred to as "Welfare Reform" (sic). The bill's stated interest was: "To replace the existing Federal Welfare programs with a single, coordinated program to seek to assure jobs, training, and income supplementation for low-income citizens in need who are not available for work by reason of disability, age, or family circumstance."

Concepts, Terms and Language

The Preamble to the United States Constitution includes the following as one of its statements of Purpose: "promote the general welfare." It is indeed part of the business of the U.S. government to do for its people what they cannot do for themselves. Clearly, H.R. 9030 recognizes that some citizens have not and cannot, even with present aid, provide adequately for themselves and their children. Most of these citizens have been and are women and dependent children, a fact voluminously documented by the U.S. Departments of Labor, Commerce, and Health, Education and Welfare – as well as multiple independent studies. The primacy of the economic needs of women and their dependent children must be the central and abiding understanding of this Testimony (sic). The needs of women and children must also be the priority focus of any humane legislation and/or programs for survival assistance if this nation ever pretends to "promote the general welfare."

It is my thesis that the ways most people, and indeed H.R. 9030, characterize poverty and the poor in this country inhibit understanding of the problems – let alone the finding of solutions. The usual language, assumptions, images and concepts impoverish people's imagination of alternative realities.

My Testimony (sic) advocates concepts, terms, and language that are apparently new and/or unfamiliar to some folks, yet these ideas are imperative for humane programs to eliminate or relieve poverty. It is precisely poverty of imagination that sanctions the acceptance of economic poverty – living below subsistence levels by some people in a nation that can afford to eliminate below-subsistence existence for anyone. Specifically, poverty of imagination helps to structure in the guarantee that women and our dependent children are the primary and majority victims of economic poverty.

Public Welfare

Let us now define public welfare accurately, identify the current beneficiaries, and create a new concept and term to eliminate the perpetuation of below-subsistence existence for some people. Public welfare is actually that public money (from men and women) which is somehow granted to citizens for some reason(s) and or purpose(s). In this realistic context, most public welfare goes to affluent or middle-income white males (it just hasn't been called *welfare*) – not to the majority of the poor who are not male, disproportionately not white, and/or not affluent, and/or not middle income. For examples of *public welfare*, mark well the following:

- Aid to needy businessmen (95% to men – mostly white) – billions of dollars annually.
- Aid to ailing railroad and airlines owners – mostly men are owners and in control.[2]
- Public Highway Aid (most poor can't afford cars to travel public highways), in lieu of Mass Transit Funds. Should poor people be called cars in order to be eligible for funded programs? (This was once suggested by writer Michael Harrington.)
- Shipbuilders' Relief – $3.8 billion annually beginning in 1970 (all men).
- Oil Producers Public Assistance Programs – $2 billion yearly from depletion allowances, recently decreased but not eliminated; the oil millionaires (U.S.) are mostly white men.
- Wealthy farmer subsidies, ie, public welfare of billions of dollars annually – mostly to men or in males' names and control through corporate agribusiness. Between 40% and 50% of the nation's impoverished are rural people, and the most disadvantaged of these are women and girls who are excluded from aid programs, who are still often denied equal ownership of capital accumulated jointly with their men/husbands. These are mostly family farmers.
- Supplementary public benefits to purchasers of government bonds via tax-exempt interest. Poor people cannot afford the bonds and thus do not receive these tax-exempt public welfare benefits.
- As of 1973, $640 million of public welfare went for air traffic control and the construction of airport facilities used by owners of private airplanes. The subsidy (welfare) comes to about $3,500 per aircraft, owned mostly by affluent white men.
- Welfare benefits of about $13.7 billion a year to the one out of twelve people owning stocks, bonds and property, and paying a capital gains at a tax rate of 50% of what they would have to pay if this were earned income from jobs. Most beneficiaries are men because men own (in the sense of control) most of stocks, bonds and property.
- Subsidy (ie, Welfare) of $9.6 billion annually to homeowners (not the poor) via tax deductions for property taxes and tax exemptions of mortgage interest payments. This amount is more than twice the budget of the U.S. Department of Housing and Urban Development and more than fifty times the amount

of money spent directly on housing assistance to the poor. Most homeowners are male and/or white. Most of the poor are female and/or non-white.

With these and other examples I could cite, it is clear that the *real* welfare "crisis" and "mess" results not from assistance or welfare to the poor, but from subsidy *welfare* to the affluent and middle-income people, predominantly white males. Indeed, if one adds up all the tax subsidies (ie, *welfare)* contained in the nation's *weekly welfare check* of $14,096.68 in 1972, one learns that of the total, 31 cents (only) went to the poor, $12.52 went to those with incomes of $10,000-$15,000 a year, $229.07 to those with incomes of $50,000-$100,000 yearly, and $13,854.78 to millionaires.[3]

Concern about *welfare* for the poor did not reach the status of a public issue until millions of needy and eligible poor were in general crises of hunger, malnutrition, illness and premature death. Only with the advent of the civil rights, poor people's, and the women's movements were the extent, depth and real victims of poverty "discovered." The issue then became a political football, but the needs of the poor were somewhat addressed, and many needy of and eligible for public assistance learned of their rights to aid, often for the first time. This meant increases in the public assistance rolls.

Who calls the predominantly white not-poor male recipients of *public welfare* (under other names) *welfare chislers* and *frauds?* In 1972, the Internal Revenue Service estimated that 34% of private interest income goes unreported compared to 3% of taxable salary income. During the same year, the U.S. Department of Health, Education and Welfare reported the incidence of fraud among the poor was *actually* only four-tenths of one percent. For true *welfare reform*, I recommend that those never poor, that those insensitive to human need:

- get the middle income and rich off *public welfare,*
- do some homework about basic causes (white, capitalist patriarchy) of poverty, and
- stop expecting only the poor to practice unsubsidized free enterprise.

A major step toward ending the poverty of the truly needy; of ending the real crisis of most *public welfare* going to those not poor; of true *welfare reform* is: ending the poverty of imagination so we may reconceptualize public assistance "to promote the general welfare." The first concept and term to introduce is *survival assistance* in lieu of the term 'welfare.' Survival assistance is more accurately descriptive of the amount and kind of public assistance this nation currently appears mature enough to share with its poor. 'Welfare' quite literally means the state of faring well and of well-being. So far, that is reserved only for those of middle or higher income. We must recognize that survival assistance is what legislation and public programs are likely to address.

Head of Household and Economic Power

The next concept and phraseology to which we must apply an enriched imagination is: "head of household." It's an anachronism whose extinction is well deserved. The term has always been problematic for women (thus producing problems for families) who believe that marriage should be an equal partnership. Further, the U.S. Census Bureau has assumed that merely being an adult male automatically entitles the male to the title "head of household," with consequent authority and decision prerogatives. Whether or not a given male exercises those privileges, the assumption of the existence of the privilege means that women's second-class status is automatically reinforced in the home and learned by children of both sexes – and learned very young.

Feminists have long noted that the nuclear family is literally the home and hotbed of much of the pathology of patriarchy.[4] The "head of household" notion in a home including an adult woman and man is antithetical to interrelationships of equality (equality of rights and responsibilities). The term implicitly or explicitly assumes that being the sole or major economic provider (if one is male, but not necessarily if one is female) entitles one to authority and decision prerogatives. Whether or not the individual exercises such privileges, their very existence jeopardizes real or potential autonomy and options of those not providing the sole or major economic support. Furthermore, economic power is thus implicitly and/or explicitly more valued than housework/maintainance support, child care contributions, socio-psychological support – all assumed to be contributed by the spouse who is not the sole or major wage earner. A key issue *is* power – its definition and distribution.

Housework, emotional support, and child care are more important for our health and comfort than is recognized generally or in the marketplace except when they aren't done or are done poorly. Resistance to paying homemakers and household workers adequately or at all, and resistance to child care legislation and funding to meet national and individual needs, are cases in point of how little these functions are valued.

The increasing realization that infant and child care, house work, and *all* other jobs are learned human endeavors of and for both sexes signals the virtual end of men's and women's labels on work in and out of the home. Even the U.S. Census Bureau and the Internal Revenue Service are expected to be educable enough to end the "head of household" designation for *any* one in the 1980 Census and substitute the term economic provider(s), to stop assuming that a male presence means one is the sole or major economic provider, and to stop denying any tax benefits to women in those instances where women are the sole or major source of family income.[3] Subsuming women and children under the characteristics of the male in the family masks important variables of socio- economic data important for policy decisions.

Effect of Sexist Language

The next imperative for H.R. 9030, albeit substantially amended as I have and will detail(ed), and/or all other legislation ostensibly addressed to human needs, if the programs are to be at all humane, is to eliminate *all*, repeat: *all* sexist and *all* patriarchal language. Language not only reflects and communicates behavior; language *is* behavior. It is a powerful method to create images and to exclude accurate images about both present reality and future potential of human beings. The language of H.R. 9030 and of its September 13, 1977 Summary and Sectional Explanation is *totally sexist* in form, content and apparent intent to the advantage of males and disadvantage of females.

'He' is *not* 'she', 'his' and 'him' are *not* 'her'. 'He', 'his', and 'him' are *not* generic for individuals of either sex. To use 'he', 'his', and 'him' as generic terms when either sex is intended for reference is inaccurate, ambiguous, misleading, fraudulent and illegal. The usage of male-only referents violates the 1964 and 1972 U.S. Civil Rights laws and Federal Executive Orders and Regulations.[6] Not only are most individuals in the nation's population 'she', not 'he'; the term 'he' discriminates against women and girls by virtue of exclusion of intent and consequence.

If the Legislators and Staffs, Cabinet Department officials and White House Staffers find it too difficult or awkward to draft legislation and programs using she/he, her/his, her/him, I propose the following:

• use *she* as the more accurately generic term; *she* includes *he* while *he* does not include *she.*
• use *her* to include *his* and *him* and thus be more generic by virtue of inclusion of the majority of the population;

• study and apply the urgent sex neutral recommendations of the U.S. Commission on Civil Rights Report, *Sex Bias in the U.S. Code*. This report correctly notes that if 'man' is used as the alleged generic for all human beings of either sex, then 'woman' is seen as the other or the second sex if seen at all.[7] Again, 'woman' is more generic as reflective of the majority of the adult population and as inclusive of man, unlike the reverse.

The equality principle, embodied in laws and regulations, requires that specific laws and regulations eschew *any* language that implicitly or explicitly assigns to women, solely based on our sex; a subordinate, dependent, and/or derivative role. Both the current U.S. Code and the proposed legislation H.R. 9030 are pervaded by concepts and language that violate the equality principle by conveying the following: "that the adult world is (and should be) divided into two classes – independent men, whose primary responsibility is to win bread for a family, and dependent women, whose primary responsibilities are [presumed to be] to care for children and household."[7,p.206] Sexist assumptions, terms and phrases represent invasions of privacy on matters that are properly decisions for the individuals involved. "Government should not steer individual decisions concerning household or breadwinning roles by casting the law's weight on the side of (or against) a particular method of ordering private relationships."[7,p.206] Drafters of survival assistance legislation and programs need to learn some basic facts to clear up some present gaps in understanding. For instance, childbearing and childrearing are *not* synonymous. Childbearing is unique to women. Childrearing is a learned function; both men and women are educable and qualifiable for these parental duties. Yet, H.R. 9030 assumes only women can and should provide child care.

The now famous (infamous?) memo of a current (former) male Labor Under-Secretary which drew an ostensible "idyllic" picture of the "traditional American Family" with a male "breadwinner, supporting Mother and the Kiddies" and suggesting that incentives should be arranged to "encourage women who are single parents to remarry,"[8] reminds one of the *Dis* qualification of this official to obey and enforce civil rights laws and regulations.

There are other places in proposed legislation, H.R. 9030, where the English is actually *Man-glish*. For example, the bill refers to an individual and *his* spouse but not an individual and *her* spouse. Such reference to the male as the individual makes her (the spouse) derivative only. References in H.R. 9030 to man and wife are in violation of the equality principle; wife is a derivative term. If there's any doubt about whether wife and husband are

derivative identities, try its counterpart *not* used *anywhere* in
H.R. 9030: woman and *her* husband. In addition, the child in H.R.
9030 is everywhere referred to as *he, his* and *him*. Most children
are girls, thus *she* and *her* are accurately generic of the child
population if only one sex referent is to be used. Also, to use *he, his*
and *him* only (in terms of child population eligible for survival
assistance), quite literally excludes all girls.

Further, members of Congress and U.S. Cabinet secretaries are
all referred to in male terms in H.R. 9030 as Congress *man*, (not
Congressone or Congressperson) or as *he, his,* or *him*. Regardless
of the sex of an incumbent or the current preponderance of males
in Congress, a position and its title has *no* sex, and legislation
extends beyond present incumbency. Male-only terminology is
intolerable and illegal because it is sex discriminatory.

Finally, most of the adult poor and needy of jobs and/or survival
assistance are women, not men. Yet, H.R. 9030's references to the
client population are all male terms of *he, his* and *him* except,
interestingly, when referring to the care of children and
household work. Then 'woman' is specifically the reference word.
Obviously, the habitual use of male-only language both *distorts*
reality in general vis-à-vis the majority of the population *and* the
majority of the adult poor and those needy of survival assistance
and jobs – *women.*

Any legislation, any proposed program(s), any public official,
any member of Congress that so *distorts* demonstrated and
documented reality is *not*, can *not* be presently capable of meeting
human needs. Further, male-only language patterns obviously
inhibit, ie, prevent one from being conceptually qualified even to
perform basic problem-solving functions. Quite explicitly, those
officials and members of Congress who draft legislation whose
primary thrust is addressed to male clients when the
government's own records and studies document that the
primary needy clients for survival assistance are *women,* thereby
demonstrate that they don't read well; don't do their homework;
and can't comprehend the reality of the problems.

In that context, the U.S. Labor Department Secretary in 1974
promised to eliminate the term 'Manpower' from all Department
references and substitute Human Resources. Such action by
drafters of legislation herein discussed is relevant in the present
moment to further aid Congress and Administration officials to
become qualified to conceptualize in fully human terms.

Illegal Gender Discrimination

Aside from the legal and conceptual necessity to eliminate male-only terms and language as detailed above, there are two additional and illegal flaws embodied in the language of H.R. 9030. The following is a quote from the HEW Secretary's office:

> Here is an example of how the new program would work: The husband in a husband-wife family with two children, who could find no job, would be provided with a minimum wage job [paying $5,512 in 1978 dollars].[9,p.3]

Note that the program won't go into effect until 1981 so that 1978 dollars may well be worth even less if inflation continues and the $5,512 itself is valued less than $5000 – less than the government's own figures of the amount necessary for 2 adults and 2 children. If one can assume that a husband is male, it is clearly *illegal* sex discrimination against women, assuming a wife is a woman, to award money based on the husband finding no job. Further, it is a violation of privacy rights and the equality principle to assume it is the man's choice to be employed and the woman's choice not to be employed.

Elsewhere in H.R. 9030, the drafters resort to euphemistic language that is not sex discriminatory on its face but portends consequences to the likely disadvantage of women. This is the language of Part C, Subsidized Work and Training 'Eligible Participants' Section 951:

> (a) ...an eligible participant shall be an adult individual (1) who is a member of a household unit which includes a child and (2) who, during the six-month period preceding application for assistance under this title, was a principal earner or was the sole earner in any such household unit, or had no earned income and no other adult in such household unit had any earned income during such six-month period; but no individual in a particular household unit shall qualify as an eligible participant if another such individual is already a participant.
>
> (b) For purposes of this title, the term "principal earner" means that adult in a household unit who had the largest total amount of earned income during the six-month period preceding application for such assistance, except that another adult in the same household unit may, in lieu thereof and pursuant to regulations prescribed by the Secretary of Labor,

> qualify as the principal earner if that adult worked the largest total amount of hours during such preceding six-month period, or if the adult otherwise determined to be the principal earner during such preceding six-month period is disabled or incapacitated or otherwise not currently available for work.[10,pp.153-154]

The terms of 'eligible participants', 'principal earner' and 'sole earner' are actually euphemisms for 'adult male' for the reasons that in this patriarchal society adult males are presumed to be the principal or sole breadwinners. Further:

• the current U.S. Code language, as demonstrated earlier, makes that assumption and creates that reality;
• employers' real policies are made and they act largely on that assumption; and
• the whole conceptualization and language of the rest of H.R.9030 implicitly makes that assumption by references to an "individual and his wife," meaning that the adult male is considered the primary client, the primary one eligible.

In addition, that part of the description of principal earner as the one who had the largest total amount of earned income during the preceding six-month period also makes the male the more likely one to be eligible. I deduce this from the U.S. Labor Department's own figures that currently full-time employed women average 57% of the pay of full-time employed men. That's called "stacking the deck" and women are not "shuffling" those cards. Indeed, the Department of Labor's own estimates project that only 14% of these jobs will go to women in two-parent families.

Therefore, H.R. 9030 in this section and the foregoing context, would further give weight of law to reinforce the likelihood that the adult male (if present) *was* the principal or sole earner and should therefore continue to be the principal or sole earner independent of the intent, wishes, preferences and possibilities of the people involved. If indeed, only *one* of two adults living together is to be eligible for such public job assistance eligibility, I suggest substituting the phrase: "the one able, willing and ready to be employed" for the term "principal earner."

The woman and man in a household may *indeed* decide that the man should be the *one* to seek Subsidized Work and Training precisely for the reasons that he (*because* he is male) may receive job preference both in the private employment market *and* in this proposed illegal program. However, for other reasons, they may decide the woman should be the *one*. That is *their* choice. Anything else in law or regulation, explicit or euphemistic language of the law, program and/or regulation, represents a governmental invasion of privacy.

Further, to legislate that only *one* of the adults in a household unit is eligible for public job assistance eligibility is overt discrimination against the poor and the needy. In *no* other publicly funded jobs (and those who work at publicly funded jobs make up over one-fifth of the paid U.S. labor force) are people eligible for publicly funded jobs limited to one to a household. The President's own household violates that principle, as do countless hundreds of thousands of other household units. If middle-income and wealthier people can have two, three, four and more of a household unit work simultaneously at publicly funded jobs, why not the poorest and neediest? One more time, we see in the proposed H.R. 9030 a proposed policy document that perpetuates the crises of *welfare* subsidy to middle income and wealthier citizens, and free enterprise (with token assistance) to the poor. I resent my tax money going to perpetuate that pathology.

Finally, for this section, I must note the *complete absence* from the proposed H.R. 9030 of any mention, even token, of Federal, State and/or local Civil Rights Laws and/or Regulations regarding employment. There is no mention of Federal, State and/or Local Executive Orders for employers with public contracts and subcontracts that require prohibitions against discrimination and *affirmative actions* to assure equal employment opportunity for citizens. This absence is also tragically and totally true for the H.R. 9030 testimonies of HEW Secretary Califano and Labor Secretary Marshall, whose positions and Departments are charged with much of the enforcement of such Laws, Regulations and Orders.

Proposal for Survival Assistance Legislation

The White House administration staff, the member of Congress introducing H.R. 9030, the HEW and Labor Secretaries are, it appears, all white men as are the President and his chief domestic policy advisor. The major victims of United States poverty are women of all races, disproportionately minority (in U.S.) women, and men of minority races. This nation has had affirmative action policies, practices, and programs for white men for centuries – they just weren't called *affirmative action*. The total absence of any reference to civil rights laws, regulations, and orders demonstrates very clearly that whatever the conscious intent, white men and white male values are *demonstrably* essentially *dis* qualified to address, conceptualize, formulate, and/or implement legislation, policies, programs that have even a prayer to achieve *survival assistance,* let alone real welfare reform. Therefore, I urge that new legislation to provide survival assistance be drafted and that a new cast of characters be retained to draft the script. Much of H.R. 9030 can be relegated to the quiet extinction it so richly deserves.

My proposed legislation for survival assistance programs would include the following features:

- Employ the poor – some of whom are knowledgeable and sophisticated about the causes of and remedies for survival needs – to participate in drafting, design and implementation of revised legislation and programs. This would provide them with economic sufficiency; give hope and trust to others who are poor, and increase assurance that real needs would be addressed.
- Employ minority people, especially women, as those disproportion- ately disadvantaged. They are and would be more likely to integrate civil rights requirements into the legislation and programs than the white men who drafted H.R. 9030 and defend its potential. Employing this population would, in addition, help make credible the government's statement of concern for their welfare.
- Employ mostly women to lead, draft, design and implement Assistance Legislation and Programs. It is mostly women who are the adults in need; it is mostly women who are struggling to become economically sufficient in a patriarchal culture; it is mostly women who are hurting and feel deeply the need for change.
- All those who work on survival assistance programs will need feminist perspectives and consciousness in the context of indivisible human rights commitments, as a Bona Fide Occupational Qualification (BFOQ) for such employment. This recommendation is crucial. To the extent this BFOQ is missing, people are sexist, racist, ageist and classist and, thus, further disadvantage the needy clients of survival assistance. Criteria for determination of this BFOQ eligibility are more precise and valid than current criteria for President, Vice-President, member of Congress, economist, researcher and other publicly responsible positions.
- The compensation for the populations recommended for survival assistance programs should be commensurate with that provided for comparable skill and experience levels in civil service classifications, plus credit for the added insights gained

from life experiences as people who are poor, minorities, aged, blind or disabled, and/or women. Formal education, at whatever level, does not include these crucial experiential backgrounds.

- Any advisory, administrative, consultant committee or body should not have a majority of more than one of either sex in groups that have responsibilities for survival assistance legislation and programs. If such an excess of that majority is to be countenanced at all, then women must be predominant for reasons already amply demonstrated.
- Employ the aged, blind and partially disabled who are willing and able to contribute to the drafting, design and implementation of survival assistance legislation and pro- grams. Currently in H.R. 9030 these people are "not expected to work." To the extent that this means that they are not *required* to work, this is a positive sensitivity that I support. I urge the substitution of the word 'required' for 'expected' because it is healthier to "expect" that some of the aged, blind and disabled can and want to work. Some of that employment can be for participation in survival assistance drafting, design and implementation itself.

In very real terms of the context of this Testimony (sic), I have demonstrated that the drafters of H.R. 9030 are:

- *BLIND* to the realities of the client populations in need of survival assistance;
- *DIS-ABLE* to conceptualize the full measure of people's needs regarding survival assistance and the genuine nature of the *real welfare crisis;*
- So *AGED* in patriarchal concepts and language that present realities about existing individuals and families are distorted and future potential and ideals are ignored.

Should we thus conclude that the drafters, designers and defenders of H.R. 9030 are too blind, aged and dis-abled for us to expect them to work at all? Or shall we assist them to find other useful work for which they may be qualified in the private or public sector? Or shall we see that they receive survival assistance and not continue on *public welfare* without "contributing to the general welfare?"

The very actions of this proposal will actually help fulfill the stated purpose of H.R. 9030: Better Jobs and Income. Further, these actions will provide some hope to others that finally an Administration and Congress are beginning to recognize who needs and can best conceptualize Survival Assistance.

Provisions Needing Further Development

There are three parts of H.R. 9030 that I support in orientation. I do not support the consequent provisions of these areas. They are child care, standards of eligibility and provisions for part-time employment.

Child Care

H.R. 9030's recognition of need for child care subsidy is a plus as far as it goes and to the extent it is recognized for both parents *or* either parent *and* for children. The limitation of the subsidy to only two children suggests a population policy post facto; it does not eliminate the third, fourth and other additional children. This bill limits the resources for quality child care, meaning that the parent(s) will have to use other resources to assure child care. This is not "pro-family" as H.R. 9030 alleges. It is simply punitive. It denies human need and the investment value of additional needed subsidy and/or the value of child care work itself.

When this nation "needed" child care provisions and resources as decided by men to be in the "national interest" during World War II, the Lanham Act was quickly passed, creating child care facilities to some 1,600,000 children of women employed in war plants. Only New York City and California continued to provide public funds for child care after World War II. How ironic, in an immoral sense, that only to produce destruction could child care be seen as part of the "national interest." When child care is needed to facilitate relief of the desperate economic needs of millions of women and men and their dependent children, child care is apparently not viewed as "in the national interest" in the present nor as investment in the future.

H.R. 9030's child care need awareness is commendable; the amounts planned are grievously inadequate. Still, *whatever* child care resources are provided, it is the parent(s) herself, himself or themselves who *must* make the decisions about whether or not to opt for such child care resources. They should not be economically penalized for such decisions, *whatever* they are. This is especially true for single-parent families. In no other area of public welfare under *whatever* name does the state, (ie, the government) presume to invade the privacy of the family to dictate family child care policies and decisions as a condition of receiving public money. Even if rejecting (an) available child care program(s) means a parent will not be free to seek or accept a paid job, the resulting survival assistance must be based on economic need, not on the values or opinions of public officials. Care of (a) child(ren) and a home *is* work. It is valuable work and investment in the future (our children), even if the Labor Department currently devalues homemaking grievously. Subtle or blatant force of a parent to obtain/accept paid employment as a condition for receiving needed survival assistance when the parent wants to care for her/his own children is *involuntary servitude*, forbidden by the 13th Amendment to the U.S. Constitution.

Standards For Eligibility

H.R. 9030's stated orientation to a single coordinated approach to need for public assistance for survival is long overdue and sounds like legislation and programs with universal standards that will be based on needs. *However*, examination of H.R. 9030 reveals that once again needy folk are categorized by:

- sex,
- relationship to a household unit,
- age,
- sightedness,
- job record,
- physical and other disability rather than ability,
- job search performance,
- state officials' understanding and misunderstanding,
- "eligibility" for job participation,
- number of children, and
- single or joint parenthood.

A single coordinated approach with a universal standard would mean the only categorization would be categories of amount of need for either money and/or job assistance ...*PERIOD.*

Part-time Job Provision

The part-time job provision for single parents (and that should be clearly parents of either sex and not presumed to be women) is to be commended – and extended. Also, these jobs need to be as substantial in compensation, career potential and benefits (pro-rated) as any other similar employment experiences, and certainly not sex stereotyped. The number of part-time jobs projected in H.R. 9030 is inadequate to the present needs. One possibility in this regard is to recognize that if child care provisions and subsidies are adequate, some folks who presently seek part-time work actually prefer full-time employment.

Areas Needing Total Re-Drafting

There are specific parts of H.R. 9030 that suggest inadequacies for genuine survival assistance for needy people. These parts require re-drafting of the legislation by knowledgeable people.

Inadequate Number of Jobs Provided

H.R. 9030 does not acknowledge the reality of the numbers of people who are unemployed but employable and not counted among the unemployed because they have become too discouraged to continue the job search. The number of jobs anticipated (1.4 million) in H.R. 9030 is no way adequate. Indeed, government must be considered the employer of *first* resort – not last resort. The government must take a leadership role in translating national, urgent needs into paid employment. Then, the private sector will either organize this work in the many areas of national, community and individual needs into ongoing employment, or the public sector will continue to provide what is needed as part of its constitutional mandate "to promote the general welfare."

Patriarchal Definition of Family

H.R. 9030 categorizes families in ways that disadvantage those that do not fit H.R. 9030's apparent model of "okay families." The bill encourages, aids via job referral, job search subsidized employment, and training and rehabilitation services, *only* if one is a man or a mother without a man to support her and their children. Thus, "okay" families consist of two parents, a woman and a man, and their one or two minor children where he is the primary breadwinner and she is the primary child-care person and houseworker. This is the nuclear, patriarchal model of an "okay family," and for them H.R. 9030 is pro-family. This "model" reflects reality in only 15% of families today.[11] Other family models are: single parent families; single or both parents with three or more children; a heterosexual couple with no children, relatives living together as aunt(s), uncle(s), niece(s), nephew(s), cousin(s), grandparent(s) and/or other multi-generational units not nuclear family; two or more people simply living together as friends, ie, women, woman and man, men, and sometimes with a child or children of one or more of the household residents; a nuclear family with two parents working and needing to for survival. All but the patriarchal model are considered *not* okay families *but* are 85% of families today.

Exclusion of Single Adults and Childless Couples

Single adults and childless couples are not eligible for Public Service Employment jobs in H.R. 9030. These people make up 30% of the poor; their exclusion from eligibility for Public Service Employment jobs is unconscionable. Legislation and programs must fit people and their needs, not vice versa.

Inadequate Job Search Provisions

Job Search provisions of H.R. 9030 are alarming; this section should be totally revised. The sex discrimination against women – the majority of the adult poor and needy – is simply illegal and immoral in terms of consequences.

Not only are the additional costs of job search (eg, transportation, child care, and communication needs) *not* subsidized, but benefits are to be *reduced* during the initial eight-week job search. The Administration alleges the reduced benefits are necessary to provide "an incentive to seek and accept employment." This is an insult to the poor and/or needy. Administration officials claim to believe that these populations prefer paid employment to public assistance, yet they structure in a penalty (reduced benefits) that clearly contradicts their claim to respect for the clients. In addition to the sexism and other insults, a family breakup incentive is even added because, under H.R. 9030, if a father deserted (what if a mother deserted?), his family would immediately become eligible for the higher benefit – as long as a child under seven is present.

There are other financial incentives in H.R. 9030, like the $3,800 income disregard, the low-benefit reduction rate, the wage supplement, and earned income tax credit, to make paid work more rewarding than not working. Thus, the additional disincentive of benefit reduction is counter-productive in terms of the equality principle. This provision does not demonstrate respect for the client populations, nor does it contribute to keeping families intact, as *they* choose.

Abandonment of Current Needs Principle

Next, I want to address Title XXI; Section 2106, Available Income; Section 2108, Distribution of Available Income Over the Accountable Period of Part A; and Section 2132, Determination of Eligibility for and Amount of Payment of Part C. These provisions compound and multiply the other noted inadequacies of H.R. 9030 by the abandonment of current needs principle. This is a cruel blow to those most needy, *not* of discretionary funds – as in the case of middle income and wealthier people who receive the overwhelming amounts of *public welfare* – but of *survival assistance* funds.

The current needs principle, which is crucial to the poor, is abandoned by H.R. 9030's proposed retrospective system of accounting. In essence, this means that if an individual or family had income adequate for survival (only) within six months previous to current need time, it is assumed that the client(s) can wait two or more months for assistance or count on States' Emergency Assistance funds to help out their desperate needs. The retrospective accounting system of eligibility is unacceptable for the following substantive reasons:

- Survival (only) income from six months' previous time is simply not available at any given current time.
- Retrospective accounting assumes savings behaviors that are seldom achieved by people with at least twice the income level of people living at subsistence level.
- The retrospective accounting system would institutionalize an even longer time lag between current need and receipt of aid than already exists. That is not reform; that is retrogression.
- The Administration itself acknowledges that the retrospective accounting system is unresponsive to current needs of clients, yet is advocating its adoption. (This statement is based on my own communications with administration officials in October and November, 1977.) Emergency assistance funds will be desperately needed for unanticipated emergencies and should not be counted on. Their anticipated use should not be structured into advance planning via H.R. 9030. Besides, emergency assistance is administered by the States, a significant number of which have been documented by U.S. Government agencies and others to be *un* responsive to critical survival needs of the poor.
- Finally, retrospective accounting would badly ignore the tragic reality that even a minimal response to poverty requires the provision of income *when it is needed;* there *is* no discretionary time when survival resources are simply not available.

Discriminatory Cash Assistance Program
The Cash Assistance Component of H.R. 9030 means "women and children last." This is true because H.R. 9030's Title XXI would provide cash assistance for families with children (which, in actuality is about 95% women with children) at 65% of the current poverty line, which itself is minimal subsistence level. The aged, blind and disabled would receive 80% of the official poverty line and the benefit level for such couples equals 98% of the poverty line. One hundred percent of the poverty line should be the minimum assistance for *all.* There is absolutely no rationale

for essentially women and children to receive 15-33 percent less than others – unless they're disabled. Why then are the Administration and/or the H.R. 9030 designers trying to disable poor women and children more than poverty already accomplishes? A woman or child is no less hungry, no less in need of clothing, shelter, and other necessities because she is not blind, not aged, and/or not disabled. This is both inequitable and myopic.

In addition, HEW's own funded income maintenance experiments described in hearings before the House of Representatives' Welfare Reform (sic) Subcommittee in October, 1977, demonstrated the benefits in nutrition, health, learning ability and performance, increased education, improved morale, and mental health of recipients of adequate income as contrasted with inadequate-income recipients. The cost effectiveness of programs publicly funded is a rightful concern of government. Are not this Administration, the drafters of H.R. 9030, educable about the immediate and future prices of being penny wise and pound foolish?

The H.R. 9030 categorization of the poor and provision of differential benefits on grounds other than need could be challenged on constitutional grounds. On December 8, 1977, the American Civil Liberties Union (ACLU) Board of Directors took the following action by majority of Board vote:

> The ACLU and its affiliates recognize and urge that the denial of benefits necessary to the basic sustenance of life of some persons, while comparable benefits are afforded by government to others, has constitutional significance insofar as the requirements of equal protection and due process are concerned ...Put another way, classifications which exclude some people from the basic necessities of life while granting such necessities to others are constitutionally suspect.[12,p.3]

Illegality and Affirmative Inaction of H.R. 9030

The approach, philosophy and proposed administration of H.R. 9030 demonstrates blatantly illegal affirmative inaction. The following sections illustrate how this is so – just for openers.

Disregard of National Women's Conference Recommendations

November 18-21, 1977, at an historic National Women's Conference in Houston, Texas, the overwhelming majority (estimated 80%) of Delegates approved resolutions on Women,

Welfare and Poverty, and on Employment. It should be noted that, in compliance with P.L. 94-167 that provided funding for this Conference and the 56 preceding State and Territorial meetings, the Delegates were demographically representative of women based on age, income level, race, geography, ethnicity and religion according to the latest available U.S. census and population data. Neither Congress nor Administration officials involved in H.R. 9030 drafting and design even begin to approximate this demographic profile – indeed most all are white men who appear to need the education available to them from the various documents of the National Women's Conference.[13] The parts of the resolutions most relevant to proposed H.R. 9030:

> **On Women, Welfare and Poverty:** ...We oppose the Carter Administration proposal for Welfare Reform (H.R. 9030) which among other things eliminates food stamps, threatens to eliminate CETA [Comprehensive Employment and Training Act of 1973] training and CETA jobs paying more than minimum wage, and does not guarantee adequate day care. We oppose proposals for "workfare" where welfare mothers would be forced to "work off" their grants which is work without wage, without fringe benefits or bargaining rights, and without dignity. H.R. 9030 further requires those individuals and families without income to wait weeks, possibly months before even the inadequate grant is available.
>
> We strongly support a welfare reform program *developed from on-going consultation with persons who will be impacted.* [emphasis mine][13,p.93]
>
> **Employment:** ...Federal laws prohibiting discrimination in employment should be extended to include the legislative branch of the federal government ...[and I would add the White House staff part of the Executive Branch.]
>
> The Congress should amend the Veteran Preference Act of 1944 (58 Stat. 387, Chapter 287, Title V, U.S. Code) so that veterans' preference is used on a one-time only basis for initial employment and within a three-year period after discharge from military service, except for disabled veterans. It should modify the 'rule of three' so that equally or better qualified non-veterans should not be unduly discriminated against in hiring.

Title VII of the 1954 Civil Rights Act should be amended to prohibit discrimination on the basis of pregnancy, childbirth or related medical conditions [sic – these are not "medical" conditions] ...Enforcement of the Fair Labor Standards Act and the Social Security Act as they apply to household workers and enforcement of the minimum wage should be improved.

All statistics collected by the federal government should be gathered and analyzed so that information concerning the impact of federal programs on women and the participation of women in the administration of federal programs can be assessed.[13,p.42]

As an elected Massachusetts delegate to the National Women's Conference, I fully supported, and indeed would have preferred even stronger language in the foregoing Resolutions, given the poverty and desperation of millions of U.S. Women and our dependent children. On the Veterans' Preference Resolution, one might remember that more women are veterans of life-risking, life-giving and life-living phenomena, the first of which is partly consequent to national policy, than is true of military veterans and women have none of the benefits, uniform, pay, prestige, status, and/or support systems. All of the 25 substantive resolutions passed overwhelmingly by the extra-ordinarily representative National Women's Conference have implications and/or applications for addressing the poverty of 24.3 million people in the United States. Over 80% of these are women and our dependent children.

Imperative for Civil Rights Enforcement

Nothing is in H.R. 9030 that addresses the education, employment, and therefore economic problems of women consequent to sex discrimination in Vocational Education programs. Recently the U.S. Department of Health, Education and Welfare (HEW) issued interpretations of the 1976 Vocation Education amendments that would water down strong anti-sex-bias provisions. In a letter to HEW Secretary Joseph A. Califano, Jr., a coalition of 21 Civil Rights and Feminist Organizations protested the HEW "issuing interpretations of the law that skirted a requirement (of the law) that State Advisory Councils include 'women who are members of minority groups having special knowledge of the problems of discrimination and training'."[14,p.15]

An HEW Secretary and staff knowledgeable about, sensitive to, and caring about the disproportionate poverty of minorities and women would assure that knowledgeable minority women serve as Advisors, and indeed paid Consultants, for enforcement of the law even *without* the strong anti-bias provisions in the law. *With* the provisions, the weakening action is unconscionable in addition to being illegal. It is illegal because "skirting a legal requirement" means avoiding and thus not obeying a law. Disobedience of law is illegal. The HEW Secretary and Staff responsible are deserving of an administrative complaint and, if necessary, a Mandamus Action (a legal action forcing an Agency charged with enforcing the law to do precisely that). Is it any wonder that minorities and women are distrustful of white men and white male-run endeavors? Revisions of/substitutes to H.R. 9030 need Civil Rights enforcements structured into Vocational Education and *every other* component of *survival assistance* legislation and programs *by* people knowledgeable of, caring, and committed to justice in demonstrable ways.

Existing CETA Inadequacies

Title II of H.R. 9030, the Job Opportunities Program, portends still further problems, especially for women, beyond those already cited. Title II will use CETA programs for job opportunities programs and, in addition to the substantive objections to CETA plan for H.R. 9030 protested by the National Women's Conference, CETA is notably weak in enforcing prohibitions to sex discrimination, as is H.R. 9030 Title II itself. CETA programs and administrators seem to have serious difficulty recognizing the demonstrable reality that it is mostly women who are poor, who need and could seek jobs under CETA and *no* job under CETA can legally be considered either "man's work" or "woman's work." *No* job has a sex.

In early October of 1976, in Fargo, North Dakota, I spent a morning with CETA people. All but three of the 25 people were women. They had been in the program about four to five weeks. *None* of the women knew that the CETA Law of 1973 forbade sex discrimination, that no job and/or training for same could legally be barred to them based on their sex. None knew of their legal and, thus, partly economic rights as citizens of North Dakota and the United States. My sharing with them of this important information and providing resources for more information were major revelations. Those who administered the CETA program in that area were not women-haters and, indeed, seemed to genuinely care about the women. I learned that they didn't know much themselves and no one had impressed on them the relevance and importance of civil rights requirements, including prohibitions against sex discrimination and sex-typing of jobs.

In spite of the greater unemployment and underemployment of women than men in every State, my own check on CETA programs nationwide in 1975 and 1976 showed that 65.8 to 70.2 percent of CETA participants were men. Revisions or, better yet, replacement of H.R. 9030 should absolutely require CETA Prime Sponsors to develop, submit and fully implement effective Affirmative Action plans. At least in North Dakota where I visited, the CETA administration recognized the needs of women as well as men for training and paid employment.

Job Match Discrimination

H.R. 9030's Section 932, Job Search Assistance Program, is laudable on the face of it. However, part of that Job Search proposes to include a "job matching program."[9] Information available to me at the time of this writing indicates the Department of Labor does indeed have a Job Match project for which the U.S. Congress appropriated $150 million, with Sperry Univac Corporation as a prime contractor. Work on this project by Sperry Univac, the Department of Labor, and some State Employment Services has already begun. Job Match includes features that are illegal, potentially illegal, and/or problematic for women and U.S. minorities. I base that statement on 125 pages of evidence from and/or about the Job Match project data and procedures.

Before going further, let me quote from the Project description itself to define job matching and indicate why and how I am alleging the Project itself has illegal and/or problematic dimensions and potential for sex discrimination, race discrimination and age discrimination. From the Introduction: "a job matching system maintains files of job orders and applicants with the goal of pairing people with jobs to best serve applicants and employers. Information describing both job orders and applicants can be stored in computers and computers can be programmed to do the matching." There are, however, factors called "Eliminators." Quoting further from the description of the Job Match project: "These items are called 'Eliminators', as they may result in the *immediate rejection* [emphasis mine] of some orders from the match."

Now, I quote further to indicate the Item Summary of those Eliminators which are illegal and/or potentially problematic. Following are "Eliminators" from the Item Summary and for which computers can be programmed to produce "immediate rejection": *sex, age, public transportation, shift, GED* (General Educational Development), *aptitudes, physical demands, working conditions.*

Sex and *age* (the latter if applied to those between 45 and 65) discrimination (and that's what "Eliminator" means) are clearly in violation of various Civil Rights Laws and/or Executive Orders. Since the Department of Labor (DOL) itself has responsibilities to enforce some of these Laws and Orders, the Job Match Program is a travesty of justice both legally and morally on those grounds alone. The other items listed in the Summary of those items I've included have potential for sex, age and race discrimination, not boldly in the face of it but in terms of interpretation, consciousness, values, and proclivities of Univac programmers and DOL personnel. The records of both do not give women and U.S. minorities much, if any, cause for confidence. None of the items in the Eliminator Summary represent automatic or necessary (if indeed *any) dis* qualifications of populations of people for jobs. To use these as "Eliminators" is clearly disadvantageous for certain people. As a matter of fact, the actual Job Match project as initiated is having precisely that effect for women, minorities, and/or people over 45, all of whom are among the ones most needy of jobs. In addition, I have a statement from a person knowledgeable about Job Match that "the people who are candidates for Job Match are those *already* skilled." (My quotes and their original sources are confidential, real, and available to someone I would trust not to jeopardize the jobs and livelihoods of my informants. The current DOL Solicitor might be such a person. I trust the Welfare Reform [sic] Subcommittee will consult me further re: the DOL Job Match.)[15] It passeth all understanding how Job Match can be seriously or confidently included as a valid component of Job Search Assistance to many of those who most need it and who need skill training even more than skill assessment or matching.

Absence of Civil Rights Consultation

Section 954b of H.R. 9030 on Subsidized Work and Training opportunities requires the consultation of appropriate labor organizations in the development of an employment opportunities plan. That's fine as far as it goes. However, given the well-documented record of labor organizations in limited representations (if even included) of women and U.S. minorities and those populations' demonstrable needs, some additional consultations are necessary. Whether in revised H.R. 9030 or re-drafted *survival* assistance Legislation as I propose, consultation with feminist and civil rights organizations are imperative. They, too, must be notified and be afforded a reasonable time, prior to submission of a plan, to comment on the plan. Such a move could doubtless improve a plan by better serving client populations and doubtless avoid some human rights violation complaints and even lawsuits.

Qualifications of Administrative Personnel

The Administrative potential of H.R. 9030 in terms of personnel, their qualifications, client support services and cost effectiveness is not reassuring. It is not so much what is included in writing in the proposed "reform" legislation, but what is not included. What is needed are provisions that substantially reform current staffing, demographics, personnel *disqualifications*, absence of adequate client support services and consequent cost *ineffectiveness*.

In Texas, for instance, under the AFDC Program (Aid for Families with Dependent Children) in the so-called WIN Program (and 97% of the needy adults in AFDC are women), 86% of the "WIN" Administrators were retired military men. It would appear that these military men were the only *WINners* – of a *public welfare* salary plus their military pensions. That's called *double dipping* at the public trough. These men had minimal, if any, experience or training in relating to women professionally, in job development skills, in counseling the poor, in understanding the need and legal requirements that women be prepared for and referred to any and all jobs for which they were qualified or qualifiable (even if the military man thought some work was "for men only" or "for women only"), in persuading employers that women have to pay the same prices as men for the necessities of life for themselves and their children (plus the fact that equal job opportunity and equal pay for equal work are laws of the land) or in providing or arranging for client support services.[16]

In addition, and of interest in terms of cost effectiveness, a cost analysis of the Texas AFDC program demonstrated that the state annually spends $15,000 per family of four to provide only $3,600 in services – including grant, food stamps, child care, medical costs, etc. Seventy-six percent, or $11,400, goes for administrative costs of salaries, etc., generally for people who are not poor and are not women. Ms. Anguiano of the National Women's Political Caucus, testifying on this analysis of costs and real beneficiaries, notes: "Perhaps no other program so clearly exemplifies the deep rooted, harmful and dehumanizing effects of institutionalized sexism as does the current AFDC Welfare Program." [16]

Current and projected (via H.R. 9030) approaches to *survival assistance* by acts of omission, commission or both portend a further institutionalization of the sexism of donor-donee, power-powerless interrelationships. If indeed retired military men and others disqualified can't survive on publicly funded pensions or other means, then they too can apply for *survival assistance* by that name via grants or job aid.[16]

Denial of Legal Abortion Funding

H.R. 9030 includes nothing about the relevance of present or potential denial of Medicaid funds for legal abortions for the poor women who choose this. This issue is relevant to reform of public assistance programs for several reasons.

A major reason is that the President, the HEW Secretary, the Supreme Court, Congress, and some State Legislatures have *made* the issue relevant. These parties have effectively interceded to stop Medicaid-funded abortions for the poor partly for the reasons of reducing "welfare costs," ie, via Medicaid funding. Abortion fund cutoff has increased overall the cost of public funds for the poor more than Medicaid funded abortions, and beyond H.R. 9030's projected cost figures. Aside from the human costs of compulsory pregnancy and unwanted children; "If only a third of the poor women who would have had Medicaid abortions in one year bear children instead, the social service and medical costs to the taxpayer will be an estimated $200 million more than all the freely chosen abortions would have cost in the first place."[17,p.95] If two-thirds have children instead of abortions, the cost will be $400 million and if all (3/3) have children and not abortions, the cost will be $600 million. Furthermore, a continued ban on Medicaid-funded abortions means about 3 million additional individual recipients of *survival assistance* each year, a cost not calculated by H.R. 9030 or Carter and Company. So much for Carter's alleged "fiscal common sense" and "compassion."

Carter and company selectively apply the logic (illogic?) that even if something is legal, the state (government) is not obligated to fund it if "moral principles" are involved. President Carter indicates that the state (ie, government) is not obligated to fund programs even when something like abortion is legal or even to equalize opportunities (as between poor women and middle income/wealthier women) "particularly when there is a moral factor involved." Even assuming that his religion and its morality as interpreted by Carter are relevant to matters of public policy – and I do not buy that assumption – Carter applies his morality selectively "particularly when there is a moral factor involved."

To wit: Capital punishment is now determined to be legal in some circumstances; it is publicly funded and applied disproportionately to the poor and to U.S. minority men and women, yet surely there are clearly moral factors involved. Anyone notice Carter speaking out against public funding of this sometimes legal act *by* the state? Also, organized violence (ie, war) including killing of human beings, is considered legal action; it is publicly funded, yet surely and clearly there are moral factors involved – yet Carter has not proposed private funding of war and preparations for war (which I consider would be an excellent idea). Quite the contrary, he proposes budgets including that for war.

Compulsory pregnancy violates the Constitutional 13th Amendment that forbids involuntary servitude. The absence of Medicaid funds for poor women who choose/need abortions for whatever reason means either seeking cheap, possibly lethal and/or damaging abortions or compulsory pregnancy. Something *no* man can fully understand is that carrying an embryo or fetus in one's body is *work* that requires time, energy, resources as does the infant and child care after birth, still expected mostly of the mother. To force this work on poor women by absence of Medicaid funds for this legal act is compulsory work against her will. That's involuntary servitude and is forbidden by the 13th Amendment to the U.S. Constitution.

SUMMARY

On grounds of cost effectiveness, justice, free choice, selective application of individual "morality" regardless of public policy, and adherence to the Constitution – which the President is sworn to uphold – Carter and Company's H.R. 9030 simply is not acceptable. H.R. 9030, which purports to be pro-family, pro-work, pro-better jobs and income, pro-cost effectiveness, is either *selectively* pro these factors and/or actually portends consequences contrary to its own stated purposes.

H.R. 9030 is pro-family only if the family is patriarchal and nuclear. It is anti-family: with a woman as the only adult; if such is intergenerational; if the family chooses and needs to have more than one earner; if more than two children need child care; if a poor woman chooses not to carry an embryo or fetus to full term; if the family disagrees with H.R. 9030's concept of who is expected and able to work; if a family can save enough from time of employment (however modest) to carry it through waiting period for aid but not save so much that it is ineligible for public aid.

H.R. 9030 is pro-work only if work is outside the home, not housecare and child care in the home; if one is a man seeking work or secondarily a woman desperate for work and fitting all the superimposed criteria including continuation of programs that are demonstrably sexist (like CETA); if one (and her/his family) can live with the thinly veiled insults of reduced benefits allegedly to assure job search and repeat that up to eight weeks yearly if necessary; if people are desperate and compliant enough to seek/accept mostly low paid jobs of uncertain futures and without the benefits of non-clients doing similar or identical work under other circumstances.

H.R. 9030 is pro-better jobs and income only if one is in States that are grossly below documented needs for *survival assistance* and then only selectively; if the poor are not in present programs that, however modest, provide better jobs and income through CETA jobs now paying $3.60 per hour but to be reduced to $2.50 hour maximum (30% reduction under H.R. 9030); if one doesn't have an unwanted pregnancy; if one fits in and in time for the only 1.4 million public service jobs, whether or not these are ones that meet human needs and/or have any intrinsic gratifications.

H.R. 9030 is cost-effective only if one is penny wise and pound foolish. The programs try to fit people into programs, rather than design methods to meet human needs. *No* part of the projected H.R. 9030 will mean resources adequate for healthy survival, according to the DOL's own documented amounts needed for 1978, let alone the likely inflated amounts needed for 1981, when 9030 is anticipated to be operational.

H.R. 9030 does not meet its own stated goals. In addition, there is no implicit, let alone explicit, acknowledgement that the middle and upper income people, not the poor, receive most of the *public welfare* in this nation, albeit under other names, and that that reality produces the real *welfare crisis*. H.R. 9030 never suggests that the poor will be welcomed as Consultants, Administrators and Policy Makers, instead of subsidizing others often less knowledgeable and often less caring, and surely less needy for these functions. That's a backward step from a dozen years ago when anti-poverty legislation required *maximum feasible participation* of the *poor* in planning their own welfare.

The most grievous critique of H.R. 9030 is its pro-male, anti-woman bias in language, concepts, and priorities. This would be unconscionable if women and men were equally victimized by poverty. Throughout the nation and in every state, women comprise clear majorities of the poor and those who need *survival assistance* and who have day-to-day responsibility for care and support of most of the poor children. The figures in both instances range from 60-95%. Thus, H.R. 9030 is not only illegal on its face; it is misogynous and immoral in values and likely consequences.

NOTES

1. Walker, Barbara G.: *The Woman's Encyclopedia of Myths and Secrets.* Harper and Row, San Francisco, 1983.

2. It appears that Amtrak will be sold. While it is true that some middle and upper income commuters will no longer be subsidized, the greatest number of Amtrak riders are lower income people.

3. Shanahan, Eileen: "276 With Incomes over $100,000 Paid No Federal Tax in 1971, A Study Shows" *The New York Times,* April 2, 1973, p. 26. Also conversations with the author of the article. The numbers have changed some but the proportions and basic conditions continue or are worse since 1980.

4. Heide, Wilma Scott: Book Review of *Time of Transition: The Growth of Families Headed by Women* by Heather L. Ross and Isabel V. Sawhill. *Social Policy.* January-February, 1977. Vol. 7, Issue 4, pp. 62-63.

5. The Census Bureau dropped the "head of household" reference because they heard there would be organized non-compliance. The Bureau denies this to be the reason they stopped the designation. I know about the non-compliance because I was organizing it.

6. *Federal Laws and Regulations Prohibiting Sex Discrimination.* WEAL, Women's Equity Action League. 1984. National Press Building, Washington DC 20045.

7. *Sex Bias in the U.S. Code.* A report by the U.S. Commission on Civil Rights. April 1977. 1100 Vermont Avenue, Washington, D.C. 20425. U.S. Publication, out of print. This was an extensive study of the U.S. Code, which forms the basis of Federal law in this country. The Report addressed Federal laws which allow implicit or explicit sex-based discrimination. There have been some changes in some of the language of the Code, but the recommended substantive changes have not yet been made. Several task forces of first the Carter and then Reagan periods were appointed to produce these changes. The changes were on the way under Carter-Mondale, but stopped when Reagan-Bush were elected in 1980. Under pressure from feminists, work on this was re-instituted but stopped when the woman in charge took it "too seriously." On January 3, 1985 H.R. 347 "Sex discrimination in the United State Code Reform Act of 1985" was introduced in the U.S. House of Representatives. On the same date, an identical bill (#586) was introduced in the Senate. Both bills

propose to eliminate the sexist language in the U.S. Code. Both bills were referred to the Committee of the Judiciary of the House and of the Senate (as of March, 1985). Until changes in the Code are made, it continues with much sex bias against women.

8. *Welfare Reform: The Question of Women.* WEAL Washington Report. August 1977, 6:4, p. 1.

9. *Better Jobs and Income Act H.R. 9030, A Summary and Sectional Explanation.* Department of Health, Education and Welfare. Office of the Secretary, Washington, DC 20201. A Summary, 1977.

10. H.R. 9030, A Bill, "Better Jobs and Income Act" 95th Congress, First Session, September 12, 1977.

11. U.S. Bureau of the Census: "Household and Family Characteristics" Current Population Report (CPR), Population Characteristics, Series P-20, Nos. 173, 191, 200, 218, 233, 246, 258 and 276. 1974.

12. Reitman, Alan: *Memo to Board of Directors, Affiliates, National Advisory Council.* Re: Summary of Board of Actions at December 3-4, 1977 Board Meeting of ACLU. November 4, 1977. I am member of ACLU National Advisory Council and receive records of all ACLU Board actions and other actions by ACLU.

13. *The Spirit of Houston: The First National Women's Conference.* The National Commission on the Observance of International Women's Year, March 1978. The National Women's Conference was held in Houston, Texas on November 18-21, 1977.

14. "Anti-Sex Bias Rules Weakened for Vocational Education. *Chronicle of Higher Education.* December 12, 1977, 1717 Massachusetts Avenue N.W., Washington, DC 20036. Additional information from private consultations with protesting organizations' representatives.

15. I gave a copy of my Breastimony to the Assistant HEW Secretary whose office was responsible for drafting of H.R. 9030, and received *no* official response in writing. However, I received three phone calls from people in that office who read it and said the world is not yet ready for me, but that I should publish my thoughts, and *that* would contribute to getting the world ready!

16. Anguiano, Lupe (Member of National Women's Political Caucus): Testimony on H.R. 9030 on October 31, 1977.

17. Steinem, Gloria: "What to Watch for in '78." *Ms Magazine.* January 1978.

CHAPTER FIVE

FUTURE SEARCH FOR WELL-FARE

So far, this Breastimony has been a critique; it has been mostly re-active to H.R. 9030 with only allusions to alternatives in concepts, language, resources to produce better jobs and income – the ostensible purposes of H.R. 9030. This section will address pro-active resources and needs for survival assistance and job creation. Requiring changed behavior only of the poor is a phenomenon called blaming the victim. Pretending that only the poor are receiving public assistance when they have not been faring well and that others have not been faring well (at public expense) is either ignorance, dishonesty, or both – but it is not welfare reform. Alleging that this nation can't afford adequate survival assistance for all of its citizens while alleging that we can (or even should) be the world's greatest arms merchants and producers of overkill (at the expense of the poor) is sick at best and morally wrong at worst.

The most significant poverty in terms of causation of grievous economic poverty of millions is poverty of the imagination. H.R. 9030 is a prime example of the impoverishment of minds to transcend what is and to envision and author legislation worthy of U.S. creativity potential. The first reality is to acknowledge we're addressing survival assistance only because the U.S. population is not (yet) mature and secure enough to provide for the genuine wel-fare of those now poor.[1]

From War-fare to Wel-fare

To change the status quo from preparations for *war-fare* against people to preparations for *wel-fare* for people requires first demythologizing some "old husbands' tales." Contrary to U.S. Pentagon-created mythology, for every billion dollars spent on the military, 57,000 (that's 57 *thousand)* jobs could have been (or could be) created in private industry or state and local government.[2] Those 57,000 jobs would be at the average annual salary of $17,543, a fairly comfortable income for a family of four. At a salary of $8,400 or above, people are deemed ineligible for public assistance under H.R. 9030, this loss represents 119,047 jobs. At the $10,500 rate the Department of Labor deemed necessary for a family of four to live just adequately, the loss represents 95,238 jobs.

Fifteen billion dollars could be redirected from the Pentagon annual budget to *wel-fare* without endangering security, especially when one realizes the United States has enough weaponry and personnel to overkill all people in the world at least *twenty* times over. The United States is a leader in the Arms Race which in no way increases security; it simply promotes war.[3] At $8,400 annual pay per wage earner, $15 billion redirected from *war-fare* could mean 1,785,705 jobs or, if shared (halftime each for 2 earners in a family unit), 3,571,410 jobs. At the $10,500 level of adequacy, $15 billion redirected from *war-fare* to *wel-fare* would mean 1,428,570 jobs or, if shared (halftime each for 2 earners in a family unit), 2,857,140 jobs. This represents 28,570 to 171,410 jobs more than H.R. 9030 would create.

I want to note just a sample of human needs that could be addressed with the redirected resources of which the $15 billion from Pentagon *war-fare* preparations is but one example.

Safe Work Environments

A comprehensive national study by the Occupational Safety and Health Administration (OSHA) of the U.S. Labor Department revealed that one of every four U.S. workers is exposed to substances known to cause death and disease; and that only five percent of the 4,636 workplaces surveyed by OSHA had made any plans to reduce chemical exposure or improve physical plant conditions. OSHA estimates it would cost $54 billion to provide warnings and health surveillance services to the 21 million American workers exposed to health hazards. Fifty-four billion dollars seems like a lot, until one realizes that OSHA also states that this amount is *far less* than the cost of treating workers victimized by cancers and other illnesses and hazards.[4] A public education campaign using the media licensed in the public interest could provide thousands of jobs (including ones for those currently employable, unemployed and underemployed) to pressure reluctant employers into compliance with the Occupational Safety and Health Act, already a matter of national policy that would especially aid the poor including those working in the dirtiest, lowest-paying, most dangerous jobs.

Equal Educational Opportunity

Title IX of the Education Amendments of 1972 forbids sex discrimination in the nation's schools and colleges which receive federal financial assistance of billions of dollars. Women and girls are the major victims of sex discrimination via policies and practices in "educational" institutions; women and girls are the major victims of poverty and those who most need *survival assistance*. There is a positive correlation which is demonstrably cause and effect, especially when coupled with employment discrimination outside the schools as well. Title IX represents *existing* social policy via the 1972 Education Amendments enacted by Congress. Title IX is not being enforced by the U.S. Department of Health, Education and Welfare, as revealed in a major recent study by PEER, Project on Equal Education Rights. PEER is a project created by NOW, National Organization for Women, Inc., Legal Defense and Education Fund to monitor Title IX compliance in elementary and secondary schools.

The PEER report[5] is an indictment of HEW which has the funds and the power to enforce Title IX. At issue are the will, the competence and the commitment of HEW to investigate and act. Only four of 16,000 school districts were investigated in four years, though it has had 100 to 150 staff members assigned to investigation and not all school districts have required investigation so the caseload has not been excessive. Less than 54% of the Office of Education's (part of HEW) $8 million budget goes for formula grant programs. The Office of Education has the discretionary power to monitor grant recipients' compliance with Title IX and the same with Student Financial Aid programs, yet individuals, not the Office of Education have taken whatever initiative has been taken so far on compliance in these two vital areas that I would call pocketbook education of would-be "educators."

Without any additional funds to H.R. 9030 and preferably for redrafted *survival assistance* Legislation, some of the poor themselves, either qualified or qualifiable for effective civil rights law enforcement, could replace current staff of HEW and other

Agencies either unable, unwilling and/or uncaring about Civil Rights Law Enforcement. Of course, the Agency and Department heads would need to be fully knowledgeable about and committed to all Civil Rights Laws and Orders Enforcement, as would the President and Vice-President. That knowledge and commitment are not yet demonstrably documented. The President and Executive Branch of the federal government's response to and indeed leadership in the idea of redrafting *survival assistance* legislation and the actual legislation re-drafted would provide some clues as to what we could hope about eliminating, especially, institutional sexism and racism as prime causes of poverty.

Secretary of Labor Ray Marshall has repeatedly stated that discriminations are major causes of unemployment[6] and poverty, and has promised vigorous enforcement of the relevant laws and orders under the Department of Labor (DOL) jurisdiction. Most discrimination results from institutionalized policies, practices and patterns of behavior. He has been in "labor" over nine months. We are still awaiting delivery.[7]

Literacy for All

It is part of our social mores partly incorporated in existing social policy, via laws, mandating school attendance until age 16, that children become and citizens be literate. This is virtually a survival requirement in the United States and, indeed, the world. Yet, there are millions of functional and absolute illiterates in the United States today. According to the U.S. Office of Education and Children's Defense Fund, over 60% of those who are illiterate are girls and women, another cause of their disproportionate poverty.

One illiteracy cause is selective enforcement of School Attendance Laws. The Children's Defense Fund study of the Washington Research Project, including door-to-door survey of 8,000 homes, showed that children "...were kept out of school either because of their race or language, because they were pregnant, because they were handicapped or just because they were poor."[8,p.3] In other words, those most needing education, including presumably functional literacy for economic self-sufficiency, are the ones for whom mandatory attendance laws are least well enforced. Equitable enforcement of School Attendance Laws, including the process of employment of the poor themselves plus an "each-one-teach-one" literacy program, should be a part of any Better Jobs and Income program. Again, no new policy is needed; just effective enforcement of existing policy including employment and thus rewarding involvement of those most needing formal education.

Humanities for All

A creative interpretation of existing social policy, vis-à-vis the existence of the National Endowment for the Humanities (NEH) could be drafted into revised legislation on behalf of the poor who need *survival assistance.* NEH states that the central concerns of the humanities are human needs and experiences, goals and values in relation to life in the present, and that living issues might be the test of humane learning.[9] Re-form of welfare (including seeing that the poor receive most of the wel-fare) is certainly a matter of human needs, relates to life in the present, and is surely a "living issue."

'Humane' is variously defined as tender, compassionate, caring for the suffering or distressed. While humane (whose definitions are identical or similar to 'feminine') is a human trait possible for both sexes, yet the expectation of and socialization for being humane (a la "feminine" socialization) is demonstrably a more normal part of female child rearing and adult socialization. Indeed, normal male socialization downplays being humane, especially if *his* "feminine" potential is too obvious. Yet, NEH has always been chaired by a man; even the job title is given a sex: *chairman* (sic); most of NEH grant awarding panels as of 1974 were male – 85%. The Office of Management and Budget (OMB), has the authority to require that NEH panels (and other award-seeking agencies) have an equitable balance of women and men.[10]

NEH grants go mostly to men (80-85%), emphasize intellectual work of the past more than existential lives of living citizens, especially the poor, and humane has had elitist, scholarly, academic interpretations and criteria which could be euphemisms for affluent white male values. For example, go back and read the NEH statement that "the central concerns of the humanities are human needs and experiences, goals and values in relation to life in the present and that living issues might be the test of humane learning." Now, read the following from NEH Media Guidelines:

> Projects Not Eligible for Support ...2. Projects that focus on current affairs or events and that are designed to elicit a specific public response or advocate a particular program of social action or change.[11,p.13]

Welfare Reform, real or ostensible, is surely a current affair and thus apparently not eligible. Yet it relates to "human needs," relates to "life in the present" and is a "living issue." Our understanding and behaviors about wel-fare (ie, people faring well, including especially poor women and countenancing poverty in such a wealthy nation) might be a "test of humane learning." Would production of a television series that dramatized the issues, definitions, realities and possibilities delineated in this Testimony (sic) be "Eligible for Support" from NEH Media Program?

I'm thinking of a series that examined and applied feminist insights to subjects like *welfare, peace, justice, employment, freedom.* These insights are implicitly futurist. Most certainly feminism elicits responses and implies social action and change. It *is* provocative. Social problems require new perspectives for solutions. Any problem requires new perspectives for solution. If the extant perspectives or methods worked, ie, solved problems, there would be no problems. NEH current Guideline #2 for Media Program negates NEH's own statement of the alleged "central concerns of the humanities." The series I envision might *well* be ineligible for NEH support if feminism were mentioned. One could always use some euphemistic term in lieu of feminism, but then questions of one's integrity are at issue.

Wel-fare Re-form

What I would propose for redrafting of *wel-fare re-form* legislation to provide real *survival assistance* would include some Presidential leadership. For example, a directive to the National Endowment for the Humanities would be needed, requiring that NEH include "humane learning about living issues" like *welfare* as part of funding of NEH itself for at least 20% of NEH project funding. Twenty percent is about the percentage of the poorest in the United States. This would add zero to redrafted H.R. 9030 costs and would be an implementation of existing social policy. Many other wel-fare re-form programs are possible.

Recipients as Consultants

Adult public assistance recipients (usually called "welfare" people) could be employed as Administration and Management Consultants based on their successful experience in administering households of four to ten people. Their administrative experience includes matters such as nutrition, health, hygiene, child care, education, heating, cleaning, family unity, etc., in limited housing of three to six rooms often of ancient vintage, with poor city services, landlord neglect of repair needs, insults as "welfare bums" and countless other problems. Most of these Administration and Management Consultants would be women because mostly women are administering homes and families with funds of $2,000-$9,000 annually for two to ten people. These paid Consultants would advise and educate public officials to save public money. These women would surely be a great asset to Boston, where School Department officials say it is hard to get the city's thousands of teachers and custodians to agree on proper classroom temperatures and even harder to get them to remember to turn down the heat and switch off all the lights at night. "In the fiscal year ended 6/30/77, the school department alone had a nearly thirty percent increase in energy bills to $6.6 million – 13 percent more than the 17 percent rise was calculated to be warranted."[12,p.65]

In this and countless similar examples of city, state and federal government, and in private businesses and corporations, the poor, who have to administer and manage with limited resources and encounter people's emotions face-to-face, not from a safe, distanced office, have much to teach current administrators and managers. It's time that any humane and genuine welfare reform acknowledge and consult (for pay) with the many poor who daily solve or cope with problems that would literally devastate many people currently paid as administrators and managers.

Administrative Re-formation

Indeed, remembering the Texas example of $11,400 of annual administrative costs for $3,600 annually in grants and services for a family of four, and that 86% of Texas WIN administrators were retired military men, NEH programs might experiment with at least three alternative approaches:

- Simply provide the $15,000 directly to families of four (and pro-rate for other-sized families) and compare the results with matched families provided $3,600 with the balance of $11,400 used for administration.
- Anyone serving as administrators of public aid programs needs bona fide occupational qualifications (BFOQs) for such functions, either by virtue of having lived at least six months on public aid or having a simulated six months experience of administering a family of four on $1,800 and everything possible that generally accompanies such an experience;
- Feminist consciousness and insights are BFOQs to administer public aid programs, for the reasons that to the extent one is not feminist one is sexist, and thus stereotypes the sexes in countless ways including expecting girls and women to be economically and otherwise dependent.

These NEH-funded projects and others would achieve NEH-stated goals including that of making "living issues the test of humane learning" and H.R. 9030's stated goals of "Better Income and Jobs," and help build the bases for genuine *wel-fare re-form.*

Legal Rights and Responsibility Education

Remembering that poverty of imagination, especially of ostensible leaders, is one of the basic causes of economic poverty in a land of plenty, there are two major educational/political endeavors that are necessary, independent of grants, job searches, and the rest of what H.R. 9030 proposes. All of this is in the context of implementing existing policy via laws, executive orders and regulations.

First, a massive on-going, personnel in-service education program of all public officials at every level of elective/appointive office – beginning with the United States President and including the Congress and the Supreme Court – is essential. This education would be about the legal rights now available since the early 60's - rights needed mostly by the 75% of the population who are not male and/or not white and additional people of minority ethnic/religious groups plus those who are handicapped. This education would include built-in evaluations and sanctions to determine their understanding and implementation of relevant Civil Rights Laws, Affirmative Actions, and Executive Orders. This education would include women's studies and minorities' studies as compensation to correct the enormous social illiteracy of most public officials about the over 65% of our population who are not male and/or not white.

Second, the same public education as above would be provided for the rest of the population who are not public officials and suffer similar social illiteracy. If this nation were threatened with imminent attack by a foreign planet or nation out to destroy democratic principles and civil liberties, there would be a massive arming (ie, military) of this nation and every media of communication would be galvanized to educate the population to the dangers of this "foreign" ideology and takeover. Billions of dollars would be spent for defense against these potential acts of commission.

Meantime, by acts of omission, many citizens do not yet understand the potential of the minority civil rights and the feminist movements to democratize this nation and make it more whole. Many citizens do not yet have enforced basic legal, economic and educational and political rights, yet it is disproportionately these populations who are most impoverished. The connections between realized rights and resources or their absence are direct and indirect. Many of these populations themselves do not yet know what legal rights they do and do not have, and how to implement/obtain rights equal to those of most white men. I am not advocating this education as a "moral (sic) equivalent of war." I am proposing this multi-media massive education as the really moral equivalent of justice and thus greater likelihood of domestic peace from increased sharing of resources.

New Policies and New Politics

If we once overcome poverty of the imagination, there are literally thousands of steps we can take to overcome economic and spiritual poverty of our people *and* within existing social policy. What follows are but five examples of Needs and Resources for Survival Assistance and Job Creation via New Policy for which H.R. 9030 is either inadequate or counterproductive.

Public Funding of Political Campaigns. Public funding of all expenses for *all* U.S. elections is the only way the poor can be self-represented. Such a funding program would require nonincumbents to have exactly the same amount of campaign money, franking privileges, media access, and spending limits as incumbents. This program would apply to local, state, regional and national offices. Criteria of eligibility for funds and legitimacy of candidacy are possible. Work on such a program has hardly begun, but it is do-able.

Job-sharing. Any state that has ten percent unemployment would have that ten percent employed (if employable) in existing jobs shared by the employed with the unemployed. This means the currently employed would work 90% of the time and do 90% of the work and the employable unemployed would work the remainder of the time and do the remainder of the work. This would require a genuine unbiased assessment of job skills, interests, experience (paid or unpaid) of the employable population, but only for job-related factors.

Any state that created/rearranged jobs so as to provide full employment without the 10% job sharing (or whatever percentages) would not need to require the job sharing. Each state would have an inventory of work that needed doing in its state to meet human needs. The state would be most effective in these regards, of course, if and when the policy for Public Funding of political campaigns were operating, for the reasons that elected and appointed public officials would more nearly reflect demographically the U.S. population and, therefore, its needs and interests as has been overwhelmingly documented by studies of women's and minorities' records in politics.

Technical Assistance for Women. Whether or not the business of the United States is or should be business, business *is* a part of the United States' life and most businesses are small businesses. The U.S. Commerce Department has documented that the average annual income of women owner-operated firms is $10,000, which is less than the U.S. Labor department determines as adequate for a family of four at 1977 prices. Clearly, women entrepreneurs are small business owners in need of technical and financial assistance.

The Small Business Administration (SBA) excluded women from Executive Order 11625 of October 13, 1971, Coverage and Programs administered by the SBA Office of Minority Business Enterprises. Women are not the numerical but are a cultural (including power and dominance) minority. The President could amend Order 11625 to include women *and* direct the General Services Administration to amend the Federal Procurement Regulations so that women business enterprises, as well as minority ones and white male enterprises, would have opportunities to participate in performance of government contracts (that's public money). The November, 1977 National Women's Conference so resolved.[13]

Ratify the ERA. The greatest disparities in legal rights, in independent economic resources, in political power, in independent economic resources, in educational equity, in health resources and in family prerogatives among many parts of the U.S. population is that between women and men, between girls and boys, to the distinct disadvantage and impoverishment of women and girls. One measure that would help correct those injustices is the Equal Rights Amendment to the U.S. Constitution (first proposed in 1923 and then it was 147 years late). The ERA would mean equalizing about 1,500 laws and codes on the national or state level most of which disadvantage women and girls. The ERA states "Equality of Rights Under the Law Shall Not Be Denied or Abridged by the United States or any of the States on Account of Sex."

Genuine Welfare Reform Legislation would structure in the ERA's ratification recommendation and the President and the political parties would have financed effective programs. Both political parties of Democrats and Republicans and the last six U.S. Presidents have "stated" that they support the ERA.[14] These individuals and groups have the political clout to achieve the ERA if they are really committed to do so. The ERA would have direct and indirect benefits and increase the welfare of U.S. women and girls, including our economic welfare. It took over 100 years and an *unCivil* War to assure the legal equality of white and minority men via the 13th, 14th and 15th constitutional Amendments. The continued exclusion of over half the U.S. population from the basic legal document, the 200-plus year old constitution, of this alleged democracy ought to indicate how deep, pervasive and institutionalized sexism is. The connections are direct and indirect. This country has been in a constitutional crisis for over 200 years. ERA is a moral imperative and a necessary new policy for genuine welfare or any other reform. An alleged democracy can do no less.

The costs of *not* reconceptualizing legislation and redrafting legislation consistent with the values, needs and "promotion of the general welfare" to which the Constitutional Preamble binds the U.S. government and this Testimony (sic) anticipates are outlined in other sections. This nation and its people cannot afford any more poverty of imagination, any more than the poor can afford to have their poverty more deeply entrenched by governmental action. Try feminism for a triumph of justice in lieu of H.R. 9030 – a travesty of justice. [15]

NOTES

1. Keep in mind the Carter-Mondale administration, even so, was infinitely more knowledgeable, compassionate, economically sound than the Reagan-Bush folks – who subsidized the wealthy and believed in free enterprise for most of the economically impoverished.

2. Marcus, Ruth: *Arms and the Women.* A discussion paper by the (then) President of the U.S. Section of the Women's International League for Peace and Freedom, 1213 Race St., Philadephia, PA 19107, 1975.

3. *Pax et Libertas (Peace and Freedom).* Women's International League for Peace and Freedom. Annual 1977. pp.46-47.

4. "Occupational Health and Safety" *SpokesWoman.* 8:6, p.11. 53 W. Jackson Suite 525, Chicago, IL 60604. $12 individuals, $20 institutions.

5. *Report on Title IX Enforcement.* PEER (Project on Equal Education Rights) 1977. 1029 Vermont Avenue, N.W. Suite 800, Washington, DC 20005.

6. Patterson, Rachelle: "Hancock Yells Foul on Privacy: John Hancock's Life Insurance Co. Resists Department of Labor Attempted Access to H.H. Personnel and Pay Records" *The Boston Globe.* December 25, 1977, p.14.

116

7. As deserving as the 1970's administrative agencies were of criticism vis-à-vis commitment and enforcement, the Reagan-Bush agencies in the 80's didn't even believe in enforcement or the laws themselves.

8. "Feminist Named to Look After Civil Rights Enforcement" *Peer Perspective.* 3:2. July 1977. PEER, NOW Legal Defense and Education Fund Project on Equal Education Rights. 1029 Vermont Ave., N.W. Suite 800, Washington, DC 20005.

9. National Endowment for the Humanities. The Jefferson Lecture in the Humanities brochure which quotes Thomas Jefferson thusly: "The earth belongs always to the living generation." 806 15th Street N.W., Washington, DC 20506.

10. *To Form a More Perfect Union: Justice for American Women.* Report of the National Commission on the Observance of International Women's Year. Superintendent of Documents, 1975.

11. National Endowment for the Humanities Division of Public Programs Guidelines, Media Program, Washington, DC, 1976.

12. Ackerman, Jerry: "Boston Schools' Wasteful Habits," part 2 of series, What Energy War? *The Boston Globe.* December 26, 1977. p.65.

13. Women were included in the SBA in the late 70's. In 1985, Reagan-Bush and company propose eliminating the SBA to help reduce the $200 million plus deficit they created *not* by SBA funding but by militarization of most international issues.

14. In the 1980's the Republican party has opposed the ERA, and President Reagan has taken an open anti-ERA stand.

15. Or even worse, the climate of the 1980's has been to impoverish the poor even more.

CHAPTER SIX

COMMUNICATIONS:
THE FEMINIST DIFFERENCE

Language both reflects and influences how and if we perceive reality. The consequences are societal as well as individual. Sexism makes the use of language in communications difficult because of its subtle and blatant dominance/submission patterns, not only between the sexes but by infection (from this hierarchy) within each sex. The differential power means the subordinate ones are likely to deny or disguise conflict and/or quietly repress their rage; the dominant ones simply ignore, oppress or exploit it. Communications within such a milieu is dishonest, inaccurate and incomplete; it exists only superficially. Feminism eschews hierarchies because they countenance dominance and submission, not only vis-à-vis the sexes but also in regard to what are called the races, religions, nationalities, sexuality preferences, age groups and economic classes. All of these false differentials are too often, but not necessarily, hierarchal barriers to communications, and are rejected by feminism in its more radical formulation.

My concept of feminism includes recognition of conflict and conflicting views without assuming that adversarial patterns of interrelations are necessary to acknowledging and resolving conflict. Patriarchy, by its very existence, is a sanctioning of basic conflicts of interest. Its particular forms in Western "civilization" (colonization) presume adversarial human relations as the norm (not to be equated with the natural). Elimination of patriarchy as the paradigm of human injustice can liberate new norms of interrelations that include genuine communications.

Communications, a vital component of change in the human interest, is technically defined as imparting or sharing knowledge, thoughts, hopes, qualities and properties about phenomena. It is an interchange of thoughts and feelings. The *com* part of 'communication' means with, jointly, in combination. This would suggest reciprocity or reciprocal, thus mutual, exchange. Much that is called communication is imparting thoughts, information, feelings and ideas, and is not really *com* munication *until* and unless the reader, listener, viewer, observer incorporates the material, scene, sound, expression into your/her/his own being and somehow responds.

In this chapter, I will be writing about language, old and new; about broadcast media including the Fairness Doctrine; about media ethics; about print media; about the relevance of feminist communications to facilitate conflict resolution and the search for peace; about alternative programming like "Face the Feminists."

Language as Change Agency

Language represents written or oral symbols used to convey whatever one wants to share. Language shapes our consciousness; it is a tool of thought and a way of behaving or relating to others. By now, I trust that I have emphasized the unacceptability of the English which many of us call *Manglish* because in sound and content it excludes the majority of the population – girls and women. *Manglish* is acceptable only when referring only to males, either in reality or potential. Beyond rejecting *Manglish* because it is not fully human or generic as it often alleges, I am one feminist who creates words when necessary. Since all language is created by people, there is no reason to exclude living people from that creation. *Shero,* for instance is a word I would consider generic for referring to an admired person; it is generic because it includes both sexes. It can be written as 's/hero' for a while, until folks become accustomed to it and assume it includes males. The same is true for s/he, for wo/man and for fe/males, although I am less inclined to use the last one because that is more clearly biological and I have no wish to appear to deny the difference of biology. S/he and wo/man are more learned phenomena.

A word I would change is history, the branch of knowledge dealing with past events. Since most of what is called history actually is *his* story and thus, a-historical, and because the word *sounds as though* it is the story of the male only, I would create the word *ourstory* to both sound and be inclusive of both sexes. I would consign 'history' (though the word ostensibly had no sexist origins or defined intentions) to anachronistic artifacts of culture.[1]

Matriot is a word I created in 1976, our Bicentennial Year. Though I consider both matriotism and patriotism to be close to anachronisms in an interdependent world, still we need reminders that a matriot loves her country even as a patriot loves his.

Another word that apparently Jessie Bernard and I (and perhaps others) share in creating is the noun *gynandry* and its adjective, *gynandrous,* as a substitute for the typical androgyny and androgynous. This means a combination of the male and female, and it reflects the traditional sex sequence of phrases like: men and women, husbands and wives, boys and girls, which reveal some unquestioned priority. So, we have simply changed the sex-related sequencing for frankly political, changed consciousness reasons that question the priority, the dominance, the overvaluing of the male as part of the process of creating balance.

Finally, I would substitute the word 'one' for the word 'man' in contexts like the following: 'chairone', 'ombudsone', 'congressone' for the one in the chair, the one who advocates, the one in Congress and similar identifications. Clearly, chairperson is preferable to chairman for the job title, but I consider *chairone* less awkward than *chairperson.*

If I have communicated effectively in previous chapters, then insisting on feminist perspectives to create a gynandrous balance will clearly be understood to mean the valuing of women and girls as well as men and boys. Further, both "feminine" and "masculine" behavior traits and values will be acknowledged and expressed by both sexes as not only natural but normal. In addition, the "feminine" (humane) qualities of gentleness, sensitivity to human needs, compassion, intuition (which may be unarticulated perceptions), receptivity to others, honest emotionality, are in ascendency and in the human interest for both sexes and all social institutions and public policies. Selected "masculine" qualities such as assertiveness – as a matter of integrity and self-confidence, as a matter of effectiveness and boldness in imagination, as a matter of creativity – are valuable for both sexes as well as institutions and policies. This is one way feminism portends communications that are in the human interest – to redefine power, to recast the characters in leadership. Asserting especially the "feminine" qualities and the people of both sexes who embody them may be necessary for both balance and humanity's survival.

The scholarship I most value searches for and envisions possibilities for the future rather than only re-searching and delineating the historical. Communications in the human interest – by which I mean whole, balanced and human – requires feminist perspectives.

The Broadcast Media

Both radio and television are licensed by the Federal Communications Commission (FCC) in the public interest. The FCC is charged with the enforcement of the Fairness Doctrine, vis-à-vis radio and television broadcasting that is licensed in the public interest. I have met with the FCC on several occasions for purposes of their education. Only two women have ever served on the FCC and one of these has been overtly non-feminist. One man who served was mostly pro-feminist. I am not sure that most of the cast of the FCC itself, so far, has been "in the public interest." Nonetheless, with the optimism born of commitment more than experience, I would like to see the Fairness Doctrine of the Federal Communications Law interpreted, as it has never been – from feminist perspectives.

The Procedural Manual of regulations to guide the FCC is itself *unfair,* both because the language is all male and because the focus is narrowed to *a* program or presentation which mostly male broadcasters consider controversial. Consider this quote from the Procedure Manual of the FCC on the Fairness Doctrine:

> *Fairness Doctrine.* Under the fairness doctrine, if there is a presentation of a point of view on a controversial issue of public importance over a station (or network), it is the duty of the station (or network), in its overall programming, to afford a reasonable opportunity for the presentation of contrasting views as to that issue. This duty applies to all station programming and not merely to editorials stating the station's position. The station may make offers of time to spokesmen [sic] for contrasting views or may present its own programming on the issue. It must present suitable contrasting views without charge if it is unable

to secure payment from, or a sponsor for, the spokesman [sic] for such views. The broadcaster has considerable discretion as to the format of programs, the different shades of opinion presented, the spokesman [sic] for each point of view, and the time allowed. He [sic] is not required to provide equal time or equal opportunities; this requirement applies only to broadcasts by candidates for public office. The doctrine is based on the right of the public to be informed and not on the proposition that any particular person or group is entitled to be heard.[2]

Two perspectives are relevant if the FCC is to conceptualize and implement licensing of broadcasters in the public interest, ie, *all* of the public. First, the context of the Fairness Doctrine is very narrow; it refers only to a *presentation* which generally means a single program. As a matter of fact, the whole or most of the orientation of a station's broadcasting and programming may be controversial in the minds of those who are not male, not white, not affluent, and/or not exclusively heterosexual. The station decides what is controversial and *that* decision is made only in the context of "a presentation," not the overall content, focus, emphases or orientations of the station or network.

Television and other mass media convey legitimacy, apparently real, about who and what are important and worthy of attention. Others remain or become invisible. The U.S. Commission of Civil Rights has documented that the over 60% of the United States population who are women and or minorities are only "window dressing on the set." Perceptions of reality are thus distorted by publicly licensed broadcasters. Further, conflict situations and adversarial relations and events seem easier for broadcasters to convey than processes, especially cooperative, peaceful processes; thus, adversarial conflicts are made to seem more worthwhile, deserving of attention. This profoundly influences the public's conceptions and our ability to work toward peace.

When one looks at the overall picture, one can easily question or challenge the: criteria for newsworthiness, emphases on conflict happenings, pictorial potential (for TV) of events, quantitative emphases as allegedly more factual than qualitative realities, reporting of mostly what men are doing compared to token amount of time for what women are doing,[3] sex role stereotyping pervasiveness, inaccurate and inadequate portrayal of women who are over 40% of the paid work force. All of these matters – and more – are issues on which feminists could demonstrably controvert what television broadcasts as reality. All of these issues reflect both male and "masculine" biases and limitations and *are* controversial in the context of communications in the human interest, in the public interest. Yet broadcasters and the FCC have still to interpret the Fairness Doctrine in the total context of a station's or network's overall philosophies, programming, emphases, values and content. Because interpretations are limited to "a presentation," there is no impetus to a broader interpretation. This means that *both* the fairness of broadcasting and the Doctrine are more apparent than real.

The Fairness Doctrine language itself and *all* of the Procedure Manual are male in language, job titles, pronouns and orientation. This demonstrable sexist and androcentric consciousness raises serious questions about the qualification(s), understanding, capacity, commitment of the FCC and its staff themselves to be fair. Repeated meetings of feminists with both broadcasters and the FCC family, since 1970, reveal that these folks don't and can't disagree with the reality of the sexism, the male bias, or the unfairness of their language; they simply do not (yet) consider the matter important enough to warrant more than token change in practice, if that. This means that, though the unfairness is acknowledged to be pervasive, again, it is not "considered" controversial and thus is not accessible to the necessarily pervasive corrective and contrasting views via the alleged "Fairness" Doctrine. The ostensible "Fairness" Doctrine remains unfair in concept, in language, in regulations, in enforcement, in interpretation by broadcasters and the government agency funded with public money to assure the public, ie, the human interest. The competence and educability of the FCC to be fair is in serious doubt.

It is difficult to be sanguine about the FCC given the findings of the U.S. Commission on Civil Rights in 1977 in their Report *Window Dressing on the Set: Women and Minorities in Television*. This is a study which some of us from NOW began urging the Commission to make as early as 1973. The title of the Report is revealing of the findings of the study. Quoting from the Report's introduction:

> Television plays the dominant role in the mass communication of ideas in the United States today ...Television does more than simply entertain or provide news about major events of the day. It confers

status on those individuals and groups it selects for placement in the public eye, telling the viewer who and what is important to know about, think about, and have feelings about. Those who are made visible through television become worthy of attention and concern; those whom television ignores, remain invisible.[4,p.3]

The essence of this Report is that there have been significant though still token changes in television since 1966 vis-à-vis women of all races and minority men, most of them consequent to citizen activism. Because the Civil Rights Commission's legal mandate is to focus on the enforcement of federal laws and performance of federal agencies that have to do with the civil rights of citizens, much attention in its 1977 Report is directed not to broadcasters but to the FCC. Again and again, the Report documents that the FCC has been limited in its consciousness, commitment and effectiveness in its legal responsibilities to license broadcasters in the public interest. Additionally, the Report documents that any corrective actions taken by the FCC have been almost solely consequent to citizen organizations' pressure, and then reluctantly, if at all. [4]

From 1970 till 1972, NOW, with the supporting petitions of 30 other national organizations, petitioned the FCC to require affirmative action of broadcasters for women as well as U.S. minorities. The FCC itself had told broadcasters that affirmative action for minorities in the U.S. was necessary for effective change results. We told the FCC we agreed; still the FCC resisted (for one and a-half years) telling broadcasters that affirmative action also was necessary for women for effective change results. Finally, the FCC was embarrassed into changing its rules by the overwhelming documentation of need, by the public support NOW generated, and by the promise (not threat) of a mandamus action by NOW.

In 1972, the Washington DC chapter of NOW, sociologists experienced in media research and other feminists monitored station WRC in the nation's capitol and compiled the most massive report *ever* done of any station vis-à-vis the three criteria of performance for granting and or renewal of a license to broadcast: employment, community relations and programming.[5] Based on the report documentation, NOW's media task force filed with the FCC a petition to deny the license of WRC. The Equal Employment Opportunity Commission agreed with and supported NOW's findings and denial petition.

Due largely to the FCC's recalcitrance,[4,p.134-145] WRC's license was never denied, even though NOW sued the FCC, and the Equal Employment Opportunity Commission supported NOW in an amicus curiae (friend of the court) brief.[6] The FCC ruled that a hearing vis-à-vis WRC license renewal was not necessary. The Court of Appeals affirmed the FCC. WRC's license was renewed. However, the whole process, the voluminous documentation of WRC's sexism, the conciousness raised, and the publicity all generated some positive changes at WRC and elsewhere and inspired organizing for changes nationwide.[7]

Clearly, the FCC licenses stations in the broadcasters', not the public's, interest. Only one station to date – in Jackson, Mississippi – has had its license renewal denied, and that was due to racism so overt and blatant that the FCC finally acted, but only after public pressure. The situation was no worse in Jackson than at WRC. The difference was in the consciousness of the FCC, in their perception of the relative importance of racism compared to sexism, and the presence on the FCC of a black man – Benjamin Hooks – who educated the rest of the Commission.

This small sampling, out of volumes of documentation in my files and of which I have first-hand experience, is shared to provide some sense of why feminists have created multiple alternative media of communications in the human interest. With all the alternative communications from and among feminists, including a beginning radio network in 1974, television is still firmly in the hands of mostly affluent white males although women own a small television station in Bridgeport, Connecticut.

The Print Media

In contrast to what has been possible in television, feminists have been able to create alternative print media at relatively less expense than, for example, television station creation or purchase would involve. One press with which I have been most involved is KNOW, Inc., a feminist press in Pittsburgh, Pennsylvania. In 1969, 20 of us decided that *Freedom of the Press belongs to those who own the Press.* Since sharing of perspectives and information via the existing print media was even more difficult for feminists then than now, our course was clear. We simply arranged to purchase a printing press, although we could not afford it and none of us knew a thing about how to operate one. It simply needed to be done; that was the important values decision. We simply rearranged our spending decisions and made spending of any discretionary money for a KNOW press a top priority. KNOW[8] lives (thanks to a benefactor who chooses to remain anonymous) as do many other presses, publications, publishing endeavors, bookstores and the beginnings of a radio network.

Still, the existing and the establishment presses need diversified perspectives, so communications change agents must continue to contribute and participate therein to reach wider readership. Sometimes this is difficult with even the more liberal publications. I want to share as an example, one experience from personal involvement with the Bakke case. Mr. Bakke was a white male engineer who applied to the University of California/Davis Medical School in 1975 and was not accepted though he passed the admissions exams with a higher score than some of those admitted who were Blacks.

In the fall of 1977, before the Bakke case was to be heard by the U.S. Supreme Court on October 13, much was written, discussed and predicted about this case. I read every copy of the *Christian Science Monitor – a* relatively liberal paper – in 1977, including everything written about the Bakke case. By September I was very disappointed that important and relevant facts were omitted completely. The *Christian Science Monitor* never reported that *all* of those accepted for admission passed the exam. They also did not report that the University of California, as part of its affirmative action, had set aside openings in new classes for qualified minority students, and for qualified students from and committed to rural areas for practice. The "rural phenomena" were not part of the civil rights law or of executive order, but constitute a desirable social good.

I wrote a short piece and offered it to the *Monitor* as a guest article or editorial, including several items of information that they had not reported. A friend at Harvard Divinity School saw what I wrote and independently generated a petition letter from Harvard Divinity students and faculty to the *Monitor*, urging their publication of my piece before October 13. The *Christian Science Monitor* did not choose to publish what I wrote at all. No reason was given. Both the Divinity School people's letter and my cover letter were complimentary to the *Monitor* and requested the article's publication as a service to its readers.

On October 13, the Supreme Court overturned the previous decision of the California Court that had upheld the University of California's position, and Bakke was admitted to Medical School. I consider what I wrote to be communication in the human interest, and regret that the *Monitor* did not publish it (though they have published many similar guest contributions). Perhaps they prefer to solicit everything; my proffer was not solicited. If that is the *Monitor* policy, I could accept the courtesy of being so informed, even though I disagree with such a policy. I am, of course, aware that its publication might have been an implied acknowledgment by the *Monitor* that their coverage of the Bakke issue, while extensive in amount, omitted some important data and insights.

In 1977, the Associated Press (AP) published its yearly editors' and broadcasters' balloting on top news stories of the year. Here are the results in their perceived descending order of importance:

1. Coldest Weather since the Founding of the Republic;
2. The spread of international terrorism;
3. The Panama Canal treaty;
4. Bert Lance's resignation;
5. Elvis Presley's death;
6. Gary Gilmore's execution;
7. The collision of two jets at Tenerife;
8. The Administration's energy policy;
9. The capture of the suspected Son of Sam murderer;
10. The investigation of Tongsun Park's alleged influence peddling.[9,p.2]

The balloting for the top news stories of the year occurred before Egyptian President Sadat's trip to Israel on November 19, which was during the November 18-21, 1977 historic National Women's Conference (NWC) in Houston, Texas. Sadat's visit partly preempted instant coverage of the Conference. The NWC was scheduled and known in early 1977; Sadat's visit was not known about till just before it happened. Yet another example of the androcentric perspective of those who control the "news."

The NWC was the most demographically representative conference *ever* held by the United States. Most delegates were women who the States and Territories elected as delegates. Where States or Territories did not demographically represent their population, delegates were appointed for demographic representation, as the Public Law that created the Conference required. The Conference was "acclaimed at home and abroad as an unprecedented demonstration of democracy at its best."[10,p.8]

Eight thousand and five hundred people registered for the NWC; 1772 of these were delegates, 186 were alternate delegates. Twenty thousand people visited the Exhibit Hall daily for four days. Eighty-three women from 56 countries were NWC guests; 23 of these were the top women leaders from 22 countries. Nearly 1500 reporters covered the Conference; all of it was tape recorded. All the major networks and U.S. publications covered the Conference. This Conference was preceded by 56 State and Territorial meetings to propose resolutions and select delegates. The Conference was the result of a year-long series of plans, work, outreach and involvement. The majority of delegates and observers cheered the change-oriented resolutions that a relatively few of us change activists had been criticized for even *mentioning* just 5 or 10 years before.

While the 26 adopted Resolutions, singly or together, are not what I consider radical, clearly their implementation would make and require significant change in women's status and the United States social institutions and values. Yet, the AP editors and broadcasters did not view the Conference as a "top news story." Most of the items they did consider are androcentric; the affairs mostly of men, though some affect women and children. It is to laugh so we don't cry at the lack of comprehension, prescience, or awareness of what the women's movement portends. Yet, one should not be surprised at the AP's ignorance and insensitivity. According to the Equal Employment Opportunity Commission, as of December 31, 1977 males were: 85% of the Associated Press' newspeople; 90% of its news editors; 97% of its correspondents; 98% of its bureau chiefs; 100% of its assistant bureau chiefs. The EEOC has determined that the AP is in violation of the 1964 Act based on a 1973 complaint filed by the Wire Service Guild and was not even investigated by the EEOC until 1976.[11]

Given the sorry history of the Associated Press' and the Equal Employment Opportunity Commission's belated but inescapable findings, I wonder how soon we can expect any resolution of the Associated Press' illegal behavior and indeed about the conflict resolution process of communications itself.

Public Conflict Resolution

In 1977, I was appointed to the Community Dispute Services Panel by the American Arbitration Association. It has been my reading, observation and existential experience that in the conflict and dispute resolution process itself, the more feminist (in reality) its approach, dimensions and behaviors, the more effective, likely of resolution and lasting are the consequences. This means:

- eschewing "either/or" adversarial, "hard line" ultimatums and linear (only) thinking;
- the ability to accommodate gracefully without compromising principle and integrity;
- the ability to use words like 'acknowledge' in lieu of 'admit';
- the ability to move from win/lose concepts to benefits for the various parties and thus to win/win concepts;
- the intuiting of real feelings and needs of other parties as well as expressing one's own.

All these and more are "feminine" qualities of people. The positive aspects of "masculine" qualities of firmness, assertiveness, genuine self-confidence during public pressure, taking risks, active advocacy, are all valuable qualities of both sexes.

The feminist/gynandrous ethos combines these thoughts, feelings, and ways of relating so that no parties need to prove their manhood or their womanhood, but only embody their transcending humanity. Whether in homes, communities, nations and/or internationally, humankind literally yearns for the justice and peace which feminism portends and desires to communicate in the human interest.

In the past several decades, over 100 pieces of legislation have been introduced into Congress, addressed to the possibility of establishing a National Peace Academy or something similar. In 1978, one of those pieces of legislation had its greatest potential yet of passage. I looked at testimony to date on similar legislation and the list of those scheduled to testify at the January 24-25, 1978 oral hearings, and persuaded Congressone Helen Mayner, a sponsor, to invite an Ethicist friend and me to submit written Breastimony for the published Record of the hearings.[12] Our Breastimony showed how the androcentric ethos has produced competition, hierarchies, inequalities and war. We emphasized the need for ascendency of "feminine" values from both sexes in societal ethos and public policy, and the descendency of "masculine" ethos, especially of machismo. We also urged the ascendency of women as the majority of the proposed commission for the reasons that women have less investment in traditional policy and status quo orientations. For both sexes, we indicated that a feminist consciousness was crucial if alternatives to patriarchal and adversarial approaches to conflict resolution were to be even conceptualized and communicated let alone realized. Our Breastimony emphasized that depolarization of the sexes and sex role desocialization are imperative if we are serious about the power of love of ourselves and others ever exceeding the love of power over and violence to others. We supported the idea of something like a Peace Academy, but *only* on feminist/gynandrous terms. Because we believe feminism portends more potential for genuine peace than anything which others testifying included at all, we consider our Breastimony to be communications in the human interest.

Face The Feminists

It is *not* enough to invite feminists to speak or write on "women's issues" such as: the status of women, the equal rights amendment, or woman's right to control her own body and that to which it will give sustenance. Nor is it enough to occasionally invite a token woman who has credentials okayed by androcentric (that is, male-centered and male-oriented) criteria, but whose consciousness has not yet rejected institutionalized sexism. Feminism is a critique of *every* aspect of society that is patriarchal – that is, male-dominated and male-oriented. Feminists have valuable insights to share with a thinking public on *all* issues in the public interest.

When, I wonder, will broadcasters "Face the Feminists" with continuing regular programming and content by that or similar names, and provide feminist perspectives by: (1) giving adequate attention to the numerous issues articulated by feminists in the interest of women and girls, caring men and boys, and indeed, the quality of our national life, (2) inviting feminists as participants, experts, and commentators on *all* human issues. Human issues requiring a "Face the Feminists" approach include for example (only):

* international affairs;
* disarmament and peace;
* excess violence in the media;
* urban policies;
* quality and equality of education;
* law and justice;
* environmental quality;
* population choices;
* impact of technology on our lives;

- welfare reform and full employment;
- experimentation on human subjects;
- nuclear proliferation and organized violence (meaning war);
- ethics in and out of the broadcast media;
- genetics and genetic engineering;
- sexuality education;
- economic politics;
- the meaning of women's studies to end the social illiteracy of an essentially male studies posing as studies of all of humanity;
- the roles of religion in our personal and national life; religion as politics;
- and every other issue that affects the lives of people.

Let us examine the potential of television programs like "Face the Feminists." I think it could be communications in the human interest. Consider the following programs:

- Graphic, that is, visual documentation of the sexist origins of much of the world's hunger, malnutrition and starvation; as Mary Roodowsky and Lisa Leghorn have done in their revealing booklet *Who Really Starves? Women and World Hunger.*[13]
- Feminist perspectives on Watergate, Koreagate, the Vietnam experience, the Panama Canal controversy, the Mideast "Peace" saga.
- Innovative television coverage of the proposed legislation for a possible National Peace Academy.
- Exploration and delineation from a feminist perspective of the sexist origins of some dimensions of racism.
- Exploration of the changed consciousness and voluntary choices about wanting or not wanting children that are making for some of the diminution of the world's population "explosion" and are confusing to the population "experts" who haven't factored in these phenomena.
- Exposé of the corporate malpractice that is due to the "masculine mystique" and the adoring "feminine mystique" that still often sustains it. What an exciting docu-drama we could produce on that issue.[14]
- Television documentaries on the double standard in mental "illness" and mental "health" as a major public health measure that could contribute to the development and practice of a single standard of mental health, absent sex role stereotyped expectations of women and men.
- A dramatic series to explore the extent to which drug use and abuse (including alcohol) represents the symptoms of peoples'

protest and rejection of these stereotyped expectations and thus performance stress for men and the trauma of boredom for women.

- Programs that educate about the potential for non-adversarial law as communications in the human interest and explore the adversarial system of the law as an obstruction of Justice. I would hypothesize, but don't know, that adversarial law surely obstructs and masks the truth, all androcentric mythology to the contrary being precisely that.

Feminist perspectives help people of diverse backgrounds to understand many human phenomena that were previously or otherwise confusing, troubling or simply taken for granted and unquestioned. Broadcasting in the public interest, it would seem, has a dynamic opportunity to seize the moment in order to share the perspectives which feminists bring to peace, justice, freedom, relationships as well as to the future. Whether folks agree, agree partly, disagree partly or disagree, my own speaking experiences at thousands of campuses, conferences, conventions, symposia, churches, agencies, broadcast media and more, reveal that people find feminist perspectives variously exciting, provocative, visionary, dynamic, educational, prophetic, or threatening. Seldom, if ever, is a feminist perspective found to be dull or unrelated to the human interest.

Most fundamentally, I'm suggesting that "Face the Feminists" (by whatever title, although that is my preference) could represent communications in the human interest. Since my writing is oriented to focus on how feminism has made, does, and might "make a difference" in our society and world, there's no reason for the broadcast media to be deprived of participating in what feminism portends.

While I have shared in, generated, supported a considerable part of the broadcast media monitoring, education, pressure for change, and consider this vital to continue, I am not sanguine about the early development of significantly changed consciousness of most establishment media "leadership." Because I am persuaded that the broadcast media, in the meantime, does violence to our spirits and indirectly to our persons, I also think there's another necessary method to hasten broadcasting in the public interest.

Partly, what I'm about to propose results from what broadcast industry "leaders" have told me in their more honest (ie, often less sober) moments. As a conscionable act of civil disobedience (or perhaps it's really civil obedience to conscience), I think it may be necessary to disempower one network, one station at a time, of both normal and emergency power – to temporarily "pull the plug" on broadcasters without destroying equipment and facilities. The know-how exists for this action; I have explored the potential. What does not yet exist are simultaneously the know-how, the change commitments, the access, and the people with the courage to accept the consequences of such civil "disobedience." This will happen. The question is not if, only when. I do consider civil "disobedience" part of the repertoire of generating changed communications in the human interest. Therefore, I include this proposal just as I have advocated it publicly. This is not a first-choice recommendation. It is, rather, a reality check suggestion. Broadcast media "leaders" know that change agents for communications in the public interest, far from being too audacious, have yet to be bold enough to communicate that broadcast violence to the spirit far exceeds the temporary inconvenience from cessation of the power to broadcast.

Throughout my writing, it has been my intent to describe and envision profound societal and universal changes consequent to feminism. When contemplating change, the more conservative folks seem to expect disaster, while change agents appear to anticipate utopia. Neither is altogether correct, but I am optimistic about feminism's being in the human interest. I trust more in the imagination of possibilities than in the delineation of the historical, except as framework and context to share what those committed to a more humane future must yet covenant, change and accomplish.

NOTES

1. Others and I are variously credited and criticized for creating the word herstory; it had an interim consciousness-changing value.
2. Federal Communications Commission, Public and Broadcasting; (Revised Edition), Procedure Manual. Federal Register, Vol. 39, #173, Part III. M St., N.W., Washington, DC 20554. September 5, 1974.
3. *Media Report to Women.* Donna Allen, Editor. 3306 Ross Place, N.W. Washington, DC 20008. Published monthly, every issue since this Reports' initiation in 1972 has documented these facts.
4. *Window Dressing on the Set: Women and Minorities in Television.* U.S. Commission on Civil Rights, 1121 Vermont Avenue N.W., Washington, DC 20425. August 1977.

5. *Women in The Wasteland Fight Back: A Comprehensive Study of Employment Practices, Ascertainment of Community Interest, and Programming of Station WRC in Washington, DC.* National NOW Action Center, 425 13th Street, N.W. Washington, DC 20004 ($3.00). 1972.

6. The Equal Employment Opportunity Commission is the Federal Enforcement Agency for the Employment Title VII of the 1964 Civil Rights Act and the 1972 Equal Employment Opportunity Act.

7. Conversation on March 16, 1985 with Attorney Whitney Adams, former NOW Media Task Force Coordinator, 1971-1973.

8. KNOW, Inc. P.O. Box 86031, Pittsburgh, PA 15221.

9. "Severe Winter Rated Top News Story of '77." *The Boston Globe.* January 3, 1978.

10. "Update 9, Dedicated to the National Women's Conference, NWC, Volunteers." National Commission on the Observance of International Women's Year, P.O. Box 1567, Washington, D.C. 20013.

11. *Media Report to Women.* June 1, 1978, pp.1-2.

12. Haney, Eleanor Humes and Wilma Scott Heide: Joint Testimony (sic) on H.R. 9356, To Establish a National Peace Academy Commission. U.S. House of Representatives Subcommittee on International Relations. Record of Hearings, January 24-25, 1978.

13. Leghorn, Lisa and Mary Roodowsky: *Who Really Starves? Women and World Hunger.* Friendship Press in Cooperation with Church World Service, 475 Riverside Ave., NY ($5.00). 1977.

14. Television documentary treatment of phenomena such as feminist psychoanalyst Robert Seidenberg has written in his book *Corporate Wives, Corporate Casualties* (American Management Association, NY 1973) could elucidate, as Dr. Seidenberg does in his preface, that corporation "cruelty is as much out of *machismo* as malice" and that unhealthy competition (redundant?) is a learned phenomenon, so a simple change in the cast of characters, by sex, is not adequate if the script remains constant. Think how much anxiety could be removed and neuroses itself could be avoided if corporate practices were changed so that corporate families were not treated as corporate baggage and corporate families understood they weren't "neurotic" to want rootedness and their own identities.

CHAPTER SEVEN

THINKING THE THINKABLE: FROM MASCULINISM TO FEMINISM

At this point, I wonder if any reader considers the assertions quoted or written in this book as too vigorous, too radical. I am reminded of Adrienne Rich's writing:

> These thoughts occur because any vision of things-other-than-as-they-are tends to meet with the charge of "utopianism," so much power has the way-things-are to denude and impoverish the imagination. Even minds practiced in criticism of the status quo resist a vision so apparently unnerving as that which foresees an end to male privilege and a changed relationship between the sexes.[1,p.153]

Yet the way-things-are can be more precisely analyzed as: masculinist in values, predominantly male in cast of characters and androcratic in policies. Feminists have been told long and often that our concerns are peripheral and secondary matters, so much so that this static and interference nearly paralyzes. Yet, fresh perspectives and bold ideas for the world's future have not and will not come out of masculinist paradigms. Euphemisms for or avoidance of feminism deprive the world of enlightened insights and reconceptualizations.

The Unthinkable: Masculinist Ideology

The unidentified but extant masculinism affirms men and "masculine" values. Masculinism defines humane "feminine" strengths as weaknesses, as necessarily subordinate to "masculine" values for public policy – as emasculatory rather than humanizing for "real" men. Among the most terrifying consequences of real (albeit unidentified) masculinism are the preparations for and threats of nuclear war.

On November 20, 1983, American Broadcasting Company (ABC-TV) presented *The Day After* which dramatized some of the consequences of simulated nuclear attack for one geographic area of Kansas. What the film portrayed was horrible. Even more terrifying was the discussion after the film. A group of prominent white men moderated by Ted Koppel and including some of the men and kinds of values that continue to get all of us into these militaristic horror scenarios pontificated. The affluent white male club was personified. The cast of characters was profoundly undemographic; the cast of minds included what are called hawks and doves, but *all* were within the masculinist paradigm with the common premise of peace as inconceivable. They counted missiles, rockets and bombs, calculated megatonnages of destruction, prated of tactics and strategies as if weapons are toys and all this is a game without human consequences. Even the most concerned, Carl Sagan, spoke of people in abstractions of a species, a taxonomical order. The *only* show of emotion was William F. Buckley, Jr.'s vituperation of hate.

This white male club's analytical ruminations about megadeath are psychotic. Clearly, this represents suicidal and homicidal avoidance of reality, this severing of mind from emotion. It also reflects the "psychic numbing of feeling"[2] so characteristic of "masculine" socialization virtually absent any "feminine" socialization. Clearly, the male club trusts material weapons technology (usually men's work) more than social technology of negotiation (usually women's work) but both are learned behaviors.

In 1962, the late Herman Kahn wrote a book called *Thinking about the Unthinkable*.[3] One need not take the Kahns of the world seriously, but folks who ostensibly act on our behalf and use our funds *have* taken Kahn seriously. For example, Kahn was one of the architects of the pacification of civilians (euphemism for killing) in Vietnam.

I hesitate to critique one not alive to respond. However, in 1975, at the Assembly of what is called The World Future Society, a live Herman Kahn and I had an encounter. I advanced the analyses that most of his proposals and ideas (as in *Thinking about the Unthinkable*) and at that Assembly were consequences and symptoms of masculinist values and consciousness. I also noted that the world is groaning under these real and potential terrors. I proposed the possibility: What if we approached global and interpersonal problems with feminist consciousness and values, beginning with the terms of the discussion? Put most succinctly, was the violence of extreme masculinism more thinkable than the transformations portended by feminism?

The setting for this encounter was a press conference, which Kahn viewed as his private one, though other Assembly speakers were included. Kahn was literally livid. He considered my approach irrelevant and ridiculous; he considered me a non-expert. No matter how gently, thoughtfully and impersonally I phrased my alternative ideas, he apparently felt personally threatened. Clearly, masculinism, even if destructive, was more thinkable to him and some others than the radical re-orientations of feminism. He wanted me removed from the room and arrested, if necessary. The apparently self-elected president[4] of this World Future Society and some others were inclined to agree with Kahn's wishes, until I reminded them of how embarrassing it would be for them to be unwilling to even consider the future in such alternatively formulated ways.

Many thoughts went through my mind during this encounter, before and since. Kahn's and most of the others' language was *Manglish*. The limits of one's language both reflect and influence the limits of one's thoughts. At the encounter described, I was mindful of an Albert Einstein quote that I had recently seen on a t-shirt: "Great spirits have always encountered violent opposition from mediocre minds."

War is the ultimate expression of the "masculine" mystique which the "feminine" mystique has been conditioned to sustain and even glorify. Feminism advances the "feminine" as the humane, the peaceful, the thinkable, be-able and do-able. World policy-makers ignore, devalue, and/or peripheralize feminist implications at enormous cost.

Many have long intuited and increasingly document that the threat of nuclear holocaust, pro-natalist population practices, environmental pollution, increasing gaps between rich and poor (and most of the poor are women and our dependent children) are inherent in and intrinsic to the predominant masculinist and male-dominated paradigm and, thus, can *not* be solved within it. Androcentric men's love affair with technologies of destruction (boys with their toys) must be replaced with social technologies that nurture and develop life and quality interrelationships.

The Gender Gap

There is not only a gap between many women's and many men's formulation and view of issues; there is also a profound values gap whose participants, with differing perspectives, include both women and men. On the most obvious level, increasingly women are voting differently than men on a range of issues: economics, human rights, war, peace, environment, education, health care, reproductive freedom, hunger, malnutrition, family planning, poverty, tax policies, social services, and violence. The range of difference in the gender gap is from five to nineteen percent.[5,6] It began to be publicly noticeable in the 1980 elections, increased in 1982 and by 1984, the gap became a chasm or gulf in some areas. Where the gap appears to be narrowing, it is because some men are moving closer to women's positions. The Women's International League for Peace and Freedom (WILPF) has relevant advice: "Listen to women...For a *change.*" Even more portentious is: Listen to and *be* feminist women and men...for significant changes.

What accounts for the gender gap as a values gap? Fundamentally, women experience life differently than men, both publicly and privately. In government at every level, men are enormously over-represented and women are obscenely under-represented. In spite of the beginning changes consequent to the regeneration of feminism in the mid-1960's, the representative gap is one Riane Eisler calls a "political gender gulf."[7] The differential participation of women and men in the upper levels of all public institutions of economics, media, health care, education and religion, is still remarkable for its token presence of women.

Further, not only is there an enormous gulf in the amount and level of office holding between women and men, but those somehow elected to represent us actually misrepresent us. One (of many possible) recent glaring examples that dramatically demonstrates misrepresentation which has heightened the gender gap is the 1982 defeat of the proposed Equal Rights

Amendment (ERA) to the United States Constitution. Nationally, American (USA) people favored the ERA by a ratio of two to one, and an even greater ratio when people knew the content and actual wording of the ERA. Taxation without representation is tyranny. So is taxation with misrepresentation. ERA, itself, is not a single issue as sometimes alleged. Constitutional equality encompasses multiple issues and hundreds of laws and regulations that disadvantage mostly women and girls. Polls indicate that women and men support ERA about equally. However, more women than men are passionately committed to ERA, and consider it of greater importance than men, thus another source of the gender gap as a values gap.

There is still a myth in the United States that women control most of the wealth. *WRONG.* The Stockholder Action Committee of NOW determined that women actually controlled 17% of this nation's wealth as of 1972. To have material resources in one's name, often for evasive tax purposes of others, is not the same as controlling the resources. On the international level, the situation is even worse. Women do 66% of the world's work, receive 10% of the world's pay for work done, and own less than 1% of the world's property.[8] Most of the adult poor in the United States are women. Most of the absolute or functional illiterates in the United States (60%) and the world are women and girls. Most of the world's adult refugees (70%) are women. In the United States alone, girls suffer malnutrition and hunger, the greatest causes of irreversible brain damage, twice as much as boys.[9]

Not only do girls and women experience political and economic realities different than boys and men, the two sexes are normally (not naturally) socialized differently in sex-stereotyped ways. Even with the beginning changes created mostly by feminism (however artificial), girls and women are still conditioned to adjust to androcracy. A pedestal is not a platform. High heels (if any 'shoes' at all) and low status remain pathological. The notion of male omniscience was never true and is increasingly rejected by aware women and caring men, including many not yet overtly feminist.

Perhaps the largest values gaps reflected in gender gaps if not gender gulfs are in the areas of national security, national defense, war and peace. Women in general and feminists of both sexes define security differently than men in general and masculinists. Security *may* include but actually transcends military hardware and personnel. Elise Boulding, former

President of Women's International League for Peace and Freedom, international peace scholar and activist writes:

> There is a vast ignorance by male policymakers of how the world works, of the system they make plans for…Women have to be introduced into policymaking in order to change the system…If you define security as making people feel safe enough to go on to do their daily business with some pleasure and some joy, then it is women who are the security specialists. Ask them what it will take to make their nation feel secure.[10,p.2]

Reagan and the Gender Gap

The advent of Reagan and Company (I do not use the word administration because that literally means the act of ministering to and the group in power is too masculinist to nurture and minister to people) and their reign of error both cause and heighten the gender gap. They do not support the ERA. They do not support reproductive freedom and choice for women, although two-thirds of the U.S. population does. They would grant a greater right to life to an embryo and fetus than to the living woman whose body the organism inhabits. It may be the most fundamental denial of civil rights that those not at risk from pregnancy (mostly male legislators, judges and public officials) deny those at risk (all of whom are women) the self-determined choices about if and how long she shall carry and nourish a foreign body before birth and probably be the main or sole caretaker after birth. Another cause of gender gaps consequent to value gaps, you can be sure.

Other civil rights, and that includes women's rights, issues causing gender gaps include the dismal record of Reagan and Company on civil rights in employment, education, housing, legal services and public accommodations. They've cut back disproportionately on funding for the Equal Employment Opportunity Commission, the Office of Federal Contract Compliance, Women's Equity Education Act, Title IX of the Education Amendment Act of 1972, Title VI, and Education Amendment of the 1964 Civil Rights Act. U.S. Labor Department funds were reduced by 5.5%, but the Women's Bureau funds of that Department were cut not 5.5% but 28%. Occupational retraining for homemakers displaced by death, desertion and divorce has been eliminated.[11]

The single poorest segment of the U.S.A. population is elderly women – disproportionately elderly women of color. Three times as many women as men are economically impoverished. Reagan and Company tried to cut back on or eliminate social Security Supplemental Income (average $128/month). It is mostly women who depend on this. Not only are there gender gaps on these and related issues, there are racial gaps of significance as well. The U.S. Commission on Civil Rights, established to monitor the U.S. Government behaviors and records on many of these issues has had its independence virtually destroyed by Reagan and Company. The effectiveness of the Commission has been so badly impaired that on April 3, 1984 civil rights activists, feminists, Hispanic and anti-poverty advocates recommended to Congress the defunding of the Commission after December 31, 1984.[12,p.3]

There are countless other value gaps that are reflected in gender, racial and other gaps. Aid to Families with Dependent Children (AFDC) has been cut 23% in the past three years. Ninety-eight percent of beneficiaries are women and their dependent children. About one half of the working families (that's the working poor) have been cut from the program, 40% of AFDC families have had benefits reduced. Only 10% received unchanged or higher benefits. [5,pp.44-54] The meaning of the phrase "Penny wise and pound foolish" becomes obvious. Michigan and other States[13] have documented increased infant and other mortality and morbidity rates consequent to budget behaviors that feed military values and hardware and further undernourish poor people. A study of budgets is a study of values.

Legal services for and with the poor have been reduced in quantity, ie, financial support, and quality by the Reagan people. Most of the poor are women and dependent children; people of color are disproportionately poor. Since 1981, the new rules on legal services are that it may be okay to provide re-active legal aid to *one* poor person, but not to provide pro-active and often preventative work to hundreds, thousands or even millions of poor in the same or similar situation as that one poor person.[14] Thus, class action suits are forbidden. These and other new rules contradict every Reagan statement vis-à-vis efficiency and simplicity in government by proliferating rather than reducing costs and individual citizen lawsuits. These rules and behaviors also tell the poor that the law and laws are for the haves – not for the have-nots. Band aids have no healing or therapeutic power;

they merely cover wounds, if that. This is one more complex of sources accounting for the values gap particularly reflected in the views of women, people of color and/or the poor.

The reduction since January 1981 of health care and related programs disproportionately affect women and children as well. One hundred percent of the Women Infants and Children Food Program (WIC) go to women and children. Only three million of the nine million eligible were reached in 1984. Yet, Reagan's Fiscal Year '85 planned reduction of $22.5 million would cut 400,000 recipients from the program.[15,16]

Eighty-four percent of food stamp users are women and dependent children. The Reagan folks have already cut the food stamp budget and anticipate greater cuts for FY85-FY89. The elderly and/or low income Americans (mostly women) are seriously threatened by food stamp reductions as are a disproportionate number of minority people. More values gaps. In low income energy assistance, 85% of the recipients are elderly and/or women-maintained households. In FY84, only 30% of those eligible received assistance, yet the FY85 budget proposed $192 million *below* the 1983 level. The budget for Rental Housing Assistance (69% needed by women) already reduced, proposes for FY85 a 38% reduction compared to FY84. Medicare, work incentive, family planning, women's educational equity and many more programs that disproportionately affect women and/or people of color have been reduced since 1981 and even more reduction is projected for FY85 and beyond.[11] Yet more causes of values gaps. I trust I need not detail here the increases in military spending since 1981, and further increases projected for FY85 and beyond. "Military" and "masculine" are almost synonymous.

No knowledgeable person can deny that federal budget and tax changes adopted since January, 1981, hit low income families hardest while already high income families gained the most. Families with incomes of $10,000 or less yearly had, at best, a yearly savings of $20 while families with an income of more than $80,000 had a yearly savings of $8,390 or more.[17] The latter includes Ronald Reagan (Robin Hood in reverse), who paid at least (from President's salary alone) $18,000 less taxes in 1983 than in 1982, according to the Associated Press. More values gaps supported more by men than by women, more by the affluent than by the poor.

The Thinkable: Feminist Values Transformations

Violence and war do not represent intrinsic strength, toughness and/or courage but rather are an acknowledgement of *impotence* to resolve conflicts maturely and/or peacefully.[18] The process of peace-making in our homes, communities and globally is dynamic, courageous and life-affirming – not passive and weak.

Other feminist connections and implications for peace include the realities that anthropologists note that the *only* characteristics common to peaceful societies and peoples is the absence of any clear or polarized sex roles.[19] Violence is not institutionalized in those societies. Women do not have to prove our "manhood."[20] The frightful human costs of masculinism and sexual inequality to women and girls is voluminously and overwhelmingly documented. What are also emerging in increasing detail around the world are the effects of social inequality on the totality of society. No news to feminists of any century is the empirical evidence by anthropologists, sociologists, historians, archaeologists, political scientists, economists and ethicists of the fundamental positive correlation between sexual inequality and a generally unjust, unequal and violent form of social organization, denials of human rights, hierarchical and authoritarian social structure and militarism.[21] Examples come readily to mind: Nazi Germany;[22] Stalin's Russia;[23] observations of patriarchal societies that have dictators (eg, Iran, Libia, Syria and South American countries); and right-wing agendas in the USA and elsewhere such as South America.

Sweden's public policies (though not all its practices) are implicitly feminist. Sweden does not countenance poverty. Sweden has not been to war for over 160 years. Sweden's Prime Minister recommends that governments take on the depolarizing of sex roles as a major responsibility. Feminist connections? I think so. Profound values transformations that would eliminate or reduce the values gaps reflected in gender gaps also require different paradigms to view people and our worlds.

In 1983, I was one of five United States women invited to conferences in Finland with Scandinavian and Russian women. (Interestingly, *every* Scandinavian woman feared U.S. policies and practices more than those of Russia.) When the people from different political and economic systems discussed underlying values, the participants developed remarkable though not total consensus. When the Russian women reverted to communist ideology and their prepared statements, it was the patriarchs speaking in women's voices. When this was gently observed out loud by a Swedish woman and discussed in a nurturing environment, it was like a revelation to the Russian women. They began to hear feminism, not as U.S. or USSR media often convey it, as women versus men, but as new paradigms. We were invited to a follow-up conference in Leningrad in 1984. The invitation was fascinating because Russia has repeatedly harrassed, censored, arrested and exiled Russian feminists while ignoring feminists from outside the USSR.

Instead of women becoming more like men, "thinking like a woman" may be the greater compliment and strength. The ability to "think like a woman" has profound resonance for most women and some empathetic men. The implications of such thinking articulated in the public as well as the private realms portend, I think, the values transformations intrinsic to feminism for all social institutions and both sexes.

One of the feminist paradigms that is not totally new but is beginning to receive more public attention is reflected in the work of Carol Gilligan in her studies of Psychological Theory and Women's Development. The phenomena she documents include that male (only) moral development has been considered the norm, that the male (only) has been presented as if generically whole (inclusive of both sexes). When women and girls differed from the male (only) norm, then the women and girls are considered not only different but inferior.[24] It is a common practice of dominants to consider those who are different to be inferior.

Some examples of differences from Gilligan's works: Female gender identity and learning is embedded in relationships and connected with concrete responsibilities to others and, more recently, to ourselves as well. Male gender identity and learning focuses on separation from others and on (ostensible) autonomy and a balancing of rights often characterized in abstractions. In essence and in general, women value and nurture relationships while men are more likely to be wary of and often threatened by relationships and loss of control. These have enormous implications for definitions and exercise of leadership and power as well as the sex of the cast of characters.

One of many striking examples of differences observed by Gilligan was the (greater) difficulty of men compared to women vis-à-vis trust. The examples are individual but the implications also transcend the interpersonal to include intergroup and international in profound terms, realities and consequences. The current distrust level of the androcentrics of the U.S. and the USSR are terrifying when one considers the consequent militarism of both.

Not only have women's voices been silenced and privatized, which may represent unacknowledged censorship, but "feminine" values remain devalued for men and for public policy.

Jean Baker Miller cites some of hundreds of issues raised by feminists and then notes:

> This list of issues suggests a most interesting and exciting proposition: In the course of projecting into "women's domain" [my quote marks] some of its most troublesome and problematic exigencies, male-led society may also have simultaneously, and unwittingly, delegated to women not humanity's "lowest needs" but its "highest necessities" – that is, the intense, emotionally connected cooperation and creativity necessary for human life and growth.[25,pp.25-26]

Surely, feminists ultimately want to eliminate the terms 'feminine' and 'masculine' especially as sex-stereotyped and differentially valued. However, mere omission of the terms does not obliterate the pervasive and deep socialization and consequences of these conditionings. First, we must bring to public as well as private political consciousness how and why the dominant culture created these dichotomies, then we can synthesize the more positive strengths of both into a healthy human society. We must take the "feminine" strengths learned mostly by women as the normative and as the base and seeds for a possible human and humane future. We must recognize and reject the ideas and realities of domination and subordination, yet remember the valuable human skills women and other subordinates often have learned. I call this assertive nurturance which surely rejects subservience.

Dominance distorts human realities and creates a system of values that in turn governs a very distorted culture. Feminist analyses generate reinterpretations of virtually everything including the conventional division between "emotional" and "rational" faculties. All people of both sexes possess both qualities to some degree. Women's greater collective yearning for peace, while often devalued as "emotional," may be much more rational than mostly men's greater emotional and immature irrationality resulting in militarism in the east, west, north and south. Many men's frighteningly naive faith in weapons technology reflects much, including simplistic military policies often driven by availability of material technology. Rational analyses highlight the genuine need for people, especially leaders, to value and develop social technologies, relational skills, affiliational qualities. At this point in time, more women have developed these learned qualities than have men.

If and it's a big if, the aforementioned qualities are not only learned but are indeed even partly intrinsic to maleness and to femaleness, we must examine this evidence to see if "anatomy is destiny" at all for men. For example, recent research among male vervet monkeys and American fraternity members both showed sustained aggression, territorial imperative and preparation for attack when both were in the presence of males only. When some males were submissive, the neurotransmitter serotonin levels in dominant males were twice as high as those of submissive males of both monkeys and men. Males not seeing dominance behavior and/or dominants and placed with all females and young monkeys or with children (not necessarily submissive) showed serotonin levels reduced. This suggests dominance, according to the researchers, to be a male-male feedback-dependent system in males. These dominance-serotonin correlations have not yet been found in females.[26]

Surely biochemical research can be sexist in its design, interpretation and/or other ways. Yet, its raw findings may suggest a degree of biological determinism for both sexes just as studies of cultural learning can suggest a degree of cultural determinism that impacts on biology and chemistry of both sexes. Such research has tantalizing implications for concrete analyses of military and other androcratic institutions.

Dominance behaviors are often much easier, quicker, and more rewarded than nurturant values and behaviors in androcentric cultures *and* in the short run. However, women and humane values can no longer be devalued, trivialized, marginalized and/or privatized. A feminist synthesis which affirms "feminine" strengths and what positive "masculine" values that do exist must challenge and transcend the masculinist social order. [27,p.292]

Then and only then can the power of love in the sense of caring about ourselves and others begin and continue to exceed the love of power over others.

NOTES

1. Rich, Adrienne: "Toward a Woman-Centered University" in *On Lies, Secrets, and Silence: Selected Prose 1966-1978.* W.W. Norton and Co. Inc., NY, 1979, pp.125-155.

2. Lifton, Robert Jay and Richard Falk: *Indefensible Weapons: The Political and Psychological Case Against Nuclearism.* Basic Books,Inc., NY, 1982. The authors make *no* connections with "feminine" and "masculine" socialization and values and/or the sex differentials in socialization and the masculinism of the militarism they decry.

3. Kahn, Herman: *Thinking About the Unthinkable.* Horizon Press, Hearst Corporation, NY, 1962.

4. I use the term 'apparently self-elected' to emphasize the fact that this individual has been listed as president of the World Future Society since 1970 without election. Although WFS meets every four years, no elections were held in their meetings of 1971, 1975, 1979 or 1983.

5. Smeal, Eleanor: *Why and How Women Will Elect the Next President.* Harper and Row, NY, 1984.

6. Abzug, Bella and Mim Kelber: *Gender Gap.* Houghton Mifflin Co., Boston. 1984.

7. Eisler, Riane: "Politics and the Gender Gap." unpublished paper, 1984. Dr. Eisler is Co-Director of the Institute for Futures Forecasting, 25700 Shafter Way, Carmel, California 93923 and author of the forthcoming book *The Blade and the Chalice.*

8. International Labor Organization. United Nations Mid-Decade Conference of International Women's Decade Pre-Conference Report for Copenhagen, Denmark, 1980.

9. *Reports of Senate Subcommittee on Nutrition,* 1972 and 1982, U.S. Government Printing Office, Washington, DC 20502.

10. Boulding, Elise: Women's International League for Peace and Freedom, 1213 Race Street, Philadelphia, PA 19107. 1984.

11. "Inequity of Sacrifice." Coalition on Women and the Budget, c/o National Women's Law Center, 1751 N. Street NW, Washington, DC 20036 ($2.00). March 30, 1984.

12. *Civil Rights Update.* U.S. Commission on Civil Rights, May, 1984.

13. *Report of Michigan Department of Social Services,* Ann Arbor, MI, 1983.

14. "Restrictions on Lobbying by Lawyers Spur Controversy at Legal Services." *Philadelphia Inquirer,* Sunday, May 13, 1984, p.3-C.

15. *A Children's Defense Budget, An Analysis of the President's FY1985 Budget and Children.* Children's Defense Fund, Washington, DC, 1984.

16. "Budget Cuts Hurt Women." *WEAL Facts,* Women's Equity Action League, 805 15th St. NW, Suite 822, Washington, DC 20005. March 1, 1984.

17. Congressional Budget Office Report. Washington, D.C. 1983.

18. Heide Wilma Scott: "Feminist Imperatives for Peace and Conflict Resolution", Testimony (sic – Breastimony) on Proposals for National Academy for Peace and Conflict Resolution. 110 Maryland Ave., N.E., Washington, DC, 1980. p.4.

19. McConahay, Shirley A. and John B. McConahay: "Sexual Permissiveness, Sex-Role Rigidity and Violence Across Cultures." *Journal of Social Issues.* 1977, 33:2, pp.134-143.

20. Heide, Wilma Scott quoted in Lisa Leghorn, "The Economic Roots of Violent Male Culture" in *Reweaving the Web of Life: Feminism and Nonviolence.* Pam McAllister, Editor. New Society Publishers, PA. 1982, pp.195-199.

21. Eisler, Riane: "Human Rights: The Unfinished Struggle." *International Journal of Women's Studies.* 6:4, pp.326-335.

22. Konnz, Claudia: "Mothers in the Fatherland: Women in Nazi Germany." in *Becoming Visible: Women in European History.* Renate Bridenthal and Claudia Konnz, Editors. Houghton-Mifflin, Boston. 1977.

23. Rowbotham, Sheila: *Women, Resistance and Revolution.* Vintage Books, NY. 1972.

24. Gilligan, Carol: *In A Different Voice: Psychological Theory and Women's Development.* Harvard University Press, Cambridge, MA. 1982.

25. Miller, Jean Baker: *Toward A New Psychology of Women.* Beacon Press, Boston. 1976.

26. "The Chemistry of Charisma," *Science Digest.* October, 1983, p.77.

27. Ehrenreich, Barbara and Deirdre English: *For Her Own Good: 150 Years of the Experts Advice to Women.* Doubleday, Garden City, NY. 1978.

CHAPTER EIGHT

WOMEN'S WORLD: INTERNATIONAL POLITICS

My writing began with an open letter to my colleagues in higher education as a quest for our humanity. That and related quests for economic justice, for healthy care, for communications in the human interest, and for scholarship integrated with action are some of the visions of feminism in the United States. However, these visions extend beyond the world of our residential homes and institutions to the universe that is our home. Women intend to be at home in the world at large. Without imposing United States' feminism on other cultures, women are developing an international sisterhood and addressing international policies within our respective countries and between nations. I close my writing with another open letter to a friend who was a U.S. State Department official.

The letter addresses the possible composition and character of a conference of women in the United States to address international issues. The reasons for excluding men – as a compensatory act and so they would be more likely to listen afterwards than if present during the conference – are delineated. The imperative for feminist leadership and participation is addressed on the simple grounds of changed consciousness. Sample issues of power, trends, economic systems, budgeting of public money, leadership, policy participation, interdependence are suggested, all in the context of significant change. Women's being at home in the world of international policies is integral to a feminist covenant with truth for the health of us all.

September 1976

An open letter to:

The Honorable Virginia Allan
Deputy Assistant Secretary of State
   for Public Affairs of the U.S. State Department
Washington, DC   20520

Dear Virginia,

This letter is addressed to you for several reasons. First, I understand you also would like a conference of U.S. women convened to address international issues. Next, you are one of the more sensitive, knowledgeable people I know in the State Department, and one who is committed to fostering the participation of women in the State Department generally and specifically in policy decisions on international issues. Indeed, the State Department is obligated in this regard by law and Presidential Executive Order 11478. Also, as you may remember, former Secretary of State William Rogers – in a 1972 State Department Conference for Non-governmental Organizations – although obviously uneasy about my questioning, told me that increasing the significant participation of women was part of your appointment charge; this was in response to my direct question to him about State Department intentions vis-à-vis women.

As you well know, what is called "Foreign Affairs" in this country is largely a foreign affair to most women in this nation, even more than to men. Likewise, what it is like to live as a woman in this and other patriarchal cultures is a foreign affair to most male foreign policy-makers and advisors. Thus, Mr. Rogers' discomfort with my question, his failure to indicate what, if any, his own and State Department's commitments were all too normal and understandable, albeit unnatural and unacceptable. Of course the concept and phrase 'foreign affairs' is an alienating one: 'international' and/or 'global' affairs might be preferable.

I want to share some dimensions that I would consider imperative for any conference(s) you might envision. Given women's near exclusion from policy participation and advising of this government on international issues, a conference of women *only* is easily justified as a simple compensatory matter of numerical justice and corrective action.

Yet, even a conference of women only will not exclude the influence of the thoughts and writings of men, because of men's dominant existential presence in what Jean Baker Miller calls "The Making of the Mind – So Far." Miller reminds us:

> Humanity has been held to a limited and distorted view of itself – from its interpretation of the most intimate of personal emotions to its grandest visions of human possibilities – precisely by virtue of its subordination of women.
>
> Until recently, "mankind's" [literally, male and/or male-oriented] understandings have been the only understandings generally available to us. As other perceptions arise – precisely those perceptions that men, because of their dominant position, could *not* perceive – the total vision of human possibilities enlarges and is transformed. The old is severely challenged.[1,p.1]

Challenge and profound changes in perceptions, values and power phenomena are precisely what women's conferences on international issues need to be about. Because so many women have actually or apparently internalized androcentric concepts and values, conference planning requires sophisticated honesty.

Foreign policy implicitly and explicity reflects men as the presumed center of gravity. Initial conferences require, literally, women as the center of gravity of international issues to correct the imbalanced patriarchal weight. For this to happen, women with feminist consciousness are imperative as participants, along with women willing to identify and work with feminist sisters. Euphemisms for, or denials of, feminism are simply inadequate to the tasks.

To those concerned with the exclusions of men at this stage, I would address several reminders:

- Legally women haven't (yet) prosecuted women's exclusion from most U.S. cabinets and foreign policy meetings, from the Presidency and Vice Presidency, Secretary of State offices, and the U.S. Supreme Court, to name a few possibilities.[2] We may yet flood the courts and administrative agencies with legal challenges to men's exclusivity, should anyone have the audacity to question the minimal compensation represented by women-only international conferences.

- It is true that men need to be informed and educated by feminist consciousness. I would envision videotaping the conferences for later availability and immediate satellite transmissions worldwide for women and men. Men might listen to women (for a change) without typical "self-listening."[3] Other women would be strengthened by hearing and seeing women only.

- The "battle of the sexes" is allegedly generated by periodic separatedness between men and women. However, the "battle of the sexes" is clearly not avoided when women and men are together. Furthermore, women were never really "armed" for the battle, or were forced into unilateral disarmament. Conferences, and much more of and by women-only, are necessary to prepare more women to reject patriarchy, to envision and create new possibilities for equal partnerships between women and men.

- No effective movement for change ever accepts the agents of oppression as designers of change until and unless such agents accept the need for both initial self-chosen separation and real equality of terms and resources. Additionally, the oppressed look to the future for change, whereas the agents of oppression are more likely to look to the present and past and may not want change. Men who are becoming feminists understand this; the ones who don't thereby disqualify themselves anyhow.

United States' women of all races, income levels, nationalities, ethnic origins, sexuality orientations, religions or no religion, various population densities, and age ranges need to be welcomed at the proposed conferences. No pretense should be made to address situations of women in other countries, or their perspectives on international issues. This is not for lack of relatedness or empathy with our sisters elsewhere, but rather the envisioned conferences would hope to generate conferences of women elsewhere just as their meetings and actions generate U.S. women getting together.

While the U.S. State Department and other departments with international implications should be expected to fund the conferences as a genuine consultancy for new perspectives and fresh initiatives, their role should be for funding and for providing a Secretariat staff for arrangements. This could be considered initial compensation for women's exclusion, but I would accept consultancy as also accurate.

There are other funding resources that can be used to augment public funds or that can be used if the U.S. State Department is reluctant to fund what it could not control. Specifically, the men who aspire to humanism could be called on to become fund-raisers. For example, Norman Cousins of *Saturday Review/ World;* John Mack Carter, former Editor of *Ladies Home Journal* and who claims awareness of women's needs; Robert McNamara, President of the World Bank; Paul Kurtz of *The Humanist* magazine; any of the Rockefeller brothers, all of whom claim concern for integrating women into international policy-making; Senator Charles Percy who sponsored such legislation but without enforcement teeth and whose commitment to women's equality with men is more apparent than real. There are thousands of other men who claim humanism – which is impossible without feminism.

Ten million dollars is a modest minimum to anticipate for the Conferences I envision with a repeat Conference each year of four successive years for monitoring/action. The $2 million yearly could be for 1,000 participants at $1,000 average each for honorarium and expenses for one week. The other $1 million would be for: arrangements; recording, reproduction and distribution of videotapes; and action implementation.

Self-selection of participants need be constrained only by guidelines for multi-racial, multi-income representation. Otherwise first come, first served after wide publicity about opportunity. Should interest exceed resources, this could be the basis for documentation of further need. Women's participation in international affairs and policy is urgently needed and long overdue, as you well know.

It would be crucial to not only include but welcome to the conferences those with radical perspectives. Radical means going to the root or origin, – in these instances to the root of problems and opportunities on international issues. That today's radicalism becomes tomorrow's common sense was a truism for universal suffrage, social security, civil rights, democracy, withdrawal from Vietnam, family planning, etc.[4] With these conferences, we could generate a speed-up of the process so that today's radicalism becomes tonight's common sense practices. Tomorrow may be too late, just as yesterday and today are already too late for the survival, let alone vitality of countless millions of people physically or spiritually killed by patriarchy.

For those who are genuinely and understandably concerned for the consequences of "biting the hand that feeds you" (ostensibly the State Department), I would counsel: (1) token morsels are subtle tyranny, not nourishment; (2) if the hand that apparently feeds somehow prevents one from self-feeding, then that hand must be "bitten" and new hands introduced; (3) if some State Department personnel literally can't bite the hand, then they should welcome as consultants and advisors the independent constituents who can and will generate humane changes. Outsiders can often better afford loyalty to truth and covenant well-documented needs for change.

If and when, these conferences happen, what issues might be raised? What differences would it make in international affairs, in U.S. international policies, in the quality of people's lives? It would require several books to do justice to those questions. Some of the questions and answers we won't know till we begin. What follows is a small sample of possibilities that are only listed, not developed. These and other ideas could be delineated in pre-conference papers so that the conference itself would be designed for women to confer, not hear someone read a paper in linear one-way articulation.

WHAT IF all issues were considered women's issues (which they are)? Currently, women's rights are considered "women's issues" and are considered of peripheral concern to most policy-makers, and are considered substantively unrelated to other issues (which they aren't). Helvi Sipila, United Nations Secretary-General of International Women's Year, has acknowledged that one challenge of the International Women's Decade is to realize that women's issues *are* the real issues, not made to seem peripheral to so-called "real issues."

WHAT IF patriarchy and its inhumane consequences viewed from feminist perspectives were central issues of these conferences? Power and powerlessness both show potentials for corruption. Power redefined can also become power reassigned.[5] Consequences of relative powerlessness clarify women's behavior and that of other oppressed people more than androcentric studies, eg, of the psychology of women. Machismo is dangerous to individual, societal and international health. Conferences need to confront these issues explicitly, not tiptoe in fearful cop-outs. Are most adult men yet educable to these realities? I think not. Sharing tapes of this conference will help prepare them.

WHAT IF Conference participants generated feminist budget analyses of spending related to international affairs and issues? Consider the following examples:
• World Bank – the amount of funds committed to women compared to the amount committed to men.
• United Nations Conferences – funds spent on International Women's Year 1975 compared to funds for Environment, Law, Habitat, Population, Hunger.

- Armaments expenditures compared to dollars for children (currently the same amount is spent in two hours for armaments as in one year for children).
- U.S. Information Agency – amount spent on films of men's activities compared to women's activities; and of the latter, how much was spent on films of the women's movement? Are there any from feminist perspectives?
- Defense Department funding compared to funding for International Commission on Status of Women.
- Space Exploration – NASA compared to human interrelations and indivisible human rights; outer space compared to inter and inner space.
- Federal Women's Program (FWP) – amount actually budgeted in State and other Departments with programs and impacts on international affairs. FWP is a program to improve the status of women in government; most departments and FWP coordinators are part time and needn't have any expertise or experience to be appointed.
- Research – amount spent for research regarding relationships of women's subordination to illiteracy, hunger, malnutrition, and poverty in general; relationships between these problems and men's use of organized violence (war) as policy and alleged problem "solving."
- Agency for International Development – amount spent on women as compared to men in both the the United States and other countries and, for both, what programs reinforce sexism and which eliminate it and integrate women in the whole development process as determined *by* women in recipient countries.
- Human Rights Policies – while the United States has stated (not implemented) that it will not give foreign aid money to countries that violate human rights by race or religious discrimination; how much money is sent yearly to countries that violate all human rights, especially women's rights? Has any money been withheld on these latter grounds and, if so, how much and on which grounds?

This list of areas needing feminist budget analyses is suggestive and makes no pretense of being comprehensive.

WHAT IF the conference participants proposed international policy consistent with feminist values? Conferences need to examine world trends in international affairs and issues. For example, what is the effect on women of increasing power and influence of Moslems whose influence from Islam openly teaches slavery, misogyny, persecution and the glorification of war? The United States' support of, selling of arms to, and implicit embrace of these inhumane "values" is not in the human interest. Few men anywhere reject patriarchy and its inhumane consequences; those who do seldom influence or make policy. Women reject patriarchy more and influence policy even less. Not only is "woman's work never done," in international affairs, our real work has hardly begun.

WHAT IF conferences addressed and demonstrated how women's leadership ability and potential can be shared without adopting destructive male-oriented values? This might include what I call assertive nurturance of our selves and others only on humane terms; affirm women's strengths (often considered weaknesses); examine organizational structures to desexigrate occupational segregation; ask different questions, eg, not are women qualified for leadership, but are men? Does the defeminization of society and international decisions cause most of the dehumanization? What are the feminist connections between these issues?

WHAT IF these conferences provided an analysis of the relations between economic systems and masculinist values and feminist values? Would real capitalism, ie, private capital for all citizens (not an economic oligarchy) contribute more or less to feminist values than real socialism? What is the experience and evidence to date? Or are feminist values the pre-conditions for what positive dimensions there are of capitalism and socialism, for real economic development and peace to occur? What if we demythologized propaganda that military spending produces jobs, when in fact every dollar redirected from military to civilian spending produces 20 times the number of jobs (and not for destruction).[6]

WHAT IF the conferences explored the complex interrelationships of racism and sexism? How much racism is "justified" on sexist grounds, ie, alleged "protection" of white women, usually from self-defense and opportunity? What if these conferences demythologized myths about black matriarchy by the Daniel Patrick Moynihans and others who are rewarded by advising and (mis) representing this country and its states?

WHAT IF the conferences examined policy potential and implementation of: no cabinet, no public body, and no advisory body, acting on international issues having a majority of more than one of either sex in its membership? What if demonstrated commitment to indivisible human rights were a bona fide occupational qualification prerequisite for such roles?

WHAT IF these conferences resulted in a drive to place women in no less than 75% of policy roles on international health issues and programs? Women are primary health providers (over 75%) in this country. Health care is basically an interrelational phenomenon possibly augmented by technology. What if these conferences addressed the need to make nursing and medicine complementary, not subordinate and superordinate, respectively, in law and practice?

WHAT IF the conferences examined the consequences of men's conditioned denial of nurturance inclinations on policies and funding in area of health-genetics; sexuality education, reproductive behavior; population policies; among hundreds of other issues in the international arena?

Though this list of possibilities may be exhausting, it is in no way exhaustive. I would urge, indeed insist, that conferences be oriented more to change actions than to principles only and or attitudinal studies. Individuals specifically and people generally are, in fact, ultimately more accepting of faits accomplis than fantasies and ideas of change. While interrelated, public policy and practice influence private behaviors and "public" acceptance more than vice-versa. For those and reasons of relevant perspectives, feminist activists experienced in catalyzing change would be crucial participants in any conference envisioned. The first and succeeding conferences need to be honestly announced as frankly intended to re-examine our national ethos so that we may move from sanctioning the ideas and realities of an affluent white patriarchy to the directions of gynandrous, multi-cultural democracy.

Thus, Virginia, I believe the foregoing thoughts are consistent with the explicit policy of the United States in law, implicit potential in democratic rhetoric, and pledges to the world in recognition of beginning universal interdependence.

Your thoughts, as always, are welcomed; your good work is continually valued; your response is eagerly anticipated.

With Warmest Wishes,

Wilma Scott Heide

Postscript to the Foregoing Open Letter

With the inauguration of President Carter and Vice President Mondale in January 1977, Ms. Allan no longer served as a State Department official. However, the conferences we both envision are still necessary. She has approved my including this open letter to her in my writing. Further, she has made copies of the original draft and shared them with various people in the U.S. State Department.

In November 1977, in Houston, Texas, the first government-funded National Women's Conference was held after 56 prior state and territorial conferences to determine the issues to be addressed and delegates to be elected. Except that most of the about 2,000 delegates were women, a compensatory necessity and choice, it was the most demographically representative conference ever held in or by this nation. It was part of the follow-up to the United Nations International Women's Year Conference and Tribune in Mexico in 1975, where 200 resolutions were unanimously adopted by the delegates from around the world.

The Houston Conference by large majorities or almost unanimously adopted 26 important resolutions.[7] No one resolution by itself is radical. The implementation of these resolutions will require and/or the combined consequences of implementations would produce some relatively radical changes in national policy and people's lives as they would choose to exercise some new options. Only one of the 1977 resolutions addresses at all the issues I envisioned for a conference of United States women on international affairs and it does not suggest a conference.

In 1980, a mid-decade International Women's Conference and Forum were held in Copenhagen, Denmark, to assess the progress on the 1975 Mexico resolutions. No other conference presently planned envisions what I advocate, as do many others. It and much more is still necessary as part of the process of changing United States' international policy makers, the cast of policy makers and the scripts of international policy. Women and men need to be at home in the world, to share in forming and informing the living values of our world. Feminism portends that covenant with ourselves, each other and future generations.

NOTES

1. Miller, Jean Baker: *Toward a New Psychology of Women.* Beacon Press, Boston, MA. 1976.

2. The appointment of one safely androcentric woman to the Supreme Court in 1981 does not change the basic point; indeed, it reinforced the androcracy.

3. Farrell, Warren: *The Liberated Man, Beyond Masculinity: Freeing Men and Their Relationships with Women.* Random House, New York. 1974.

4. Mills, Garry: "Feminists and Other Useful Fanatics." *Harper's Magazine.* June 1976.

5. Heide, Wilma Scott: "Feminism Means She Is Risen to Redefine and Reassign Power for Life." Keynote speech at Conference on Power as Cause of War and Potential for Peace, Outlawry of War Foundation, University of Idaho, April 2-4, 1973. Reprinted by KNOW, Inc., P.O. Box 86031, Pittsburgh, PA 15221.

6. *Fact Sheet.* January 1976. Women's International League for Peace and Freedom, 1213 Race Street, Philadelphia, PA 19107.

7. National Plan of Action, National Women's Conference, International Women's Year Commission, P.O. Box 1567, Washington, DC 20013.

INDEX

Aid for Families with Dependent Children, 98; Reagan funding cuts in, 141

abortion, 46-47; funding for, 99

action: and knowledge, 70; and scholarship, 55-72

activism, political, 39

activism/thought, in health care, 50-51

activists, nurturance of, 71

actor, defined, 31n

ad-ministration, defined, 13

administration: proposed in HR 9030, 98-99; re-formation of in public aid programs, 111; use of word, 140

adversarial law, 63; proposed TV coverage of, 131

affirmative action: absence in HR 9030, 84; in higher education, 5; for white men, 84; women's studies as, 12

affirmative inaction: of HR 9030, 92-100; in the media, 123-124

ageism, and sexism, 6

Agency for International development (AID), 25-26

agribusiness: and corporate malpractice, 42; gendering of knowledge in, 25-27

Allan, Virginia, 149-150

American Civil Liberties Union (ACLU), 92

American Medical Association, 37

American Nurses' Association, 39

American Telephone and Telegraph Co. (AT&T), 67

Anguiano, Lupe, 98

Arditti, Rita, 21-22, 37

art, 15-16

assertive nurturance: as feminist transformation, 145; and health care, 51; of self-help movements, 38

Association for Women in Psychology, 41

Baker, Liva, 2-3

Bakke case, media treatment of, 125-126

battle of the sexes, 152

behavior: biological basis of, 23-25; and mental health, 40-41

bias: of androcentric scholarship, 55-56; future search of, 70; of media, 122

biology: and behavior, 23, 146; definitions of, 47; of gender, 11-12

bona fide occupational qualification (BFOQ): for employment on survival assistance programs, 85; for leadership, 58; of public aid program administrators, 111; for public roles, 156-157; for scholarship, 56

Boulding, Elise, 139-140

breastimony: defined, 73-74; on National Peace Academy, 128-129; response to on HR 9030, 103n

broadcast media, 120-124; feminist perspectives on, 129-132; see also media

budgets: analysis of, 154-155; values reflected in, 141-142; see also funding

Carter and company, 73; moral principles of, 99, 115n

cash assistance to poor, 91-92

Cassandra: Radical Feminist Nurses Network, 52n

capitalism: and economic development, 156; and health care, 35; and agribusiness, 26-27

Center for the Study of Democratic Institutions (CSDI), 65

chairone, defined, 119

change: and activism, 70-71; via education, 28-29; and feminist scholarship, 56-57; and international issues, 151-152; language as agency for, 118-120; movements for, 29; origins of, 71; women's role in, 65; see also entire book

child bearing, 46; defined, 80

child care: for education, 49; funding for, 78; provisions in HR 9030, as priority, 87-88

child rearing, defined, 80

Christian Science Monitor, 125-126

civil disobedience, proposed media action, 131-132

civil rights: absense of in HR 9030, 84; consultation by women and minorities, 97-98; differentials in, 61; enforcement of, 94-95, 108; in health care, 44; illiteracy of, 112; male-only language as violation of, 79; and the media, 121, 125-126; National Women's Conference recommendations on, 94; Reagan record on, 140; violations of by AT&T, 67

civilization, (sic) colonization, 17, 117

classism, and sexism, 6

colonization, and gendering of knowledge, 17

communications, 117-133; defined, 118; in the human interest, 128; and language, 177; to redefine power, 120

Comprehensive Education and Training Act of 1973 (CETA), 93; existing inadequacies of, 95-96

comtestive, defined, 13

conflict: feminist concept of, 117; portrayed by media, 121; impotence to resolve, 143

conflict resolution, 127-129;feminist approach to, 128

consciousness: as BFOQ, 111; and health care, 40-47; and health values, 48; and international policy, 151; and language, 118; and men, 151-152; of policy makers, 43; and population choices, 63; rape of, 9; and scholarship, 70; of sex-stereotyped dichotomies, 145-146; and survival assistance, 85; see also entire book

consultation: by feminists, 98; by women and minorities on civil rights, 97-98

consultants: recipients of assistance as, 110-111; women as, 95

control (social), and reproductive choice, 47

critical incident technique, 68

current needs principle, 90-91

Daly, Mary, 20

Dalkon Shield (IUD), 41

demystification, of knowledge in health care, 37-38

DES (diethystilbestrol), 42

desexigration, 49, 156

deviance, defined, 60

discrimination: in academia, 9; in cash assistance programs, 91-92; illegal gender, 82-84; institutionalized practice of, 9; in job opportunities, 95-97; in job search, 90; in language, 81; in media, 122-124; regulations against in education, 107; in schools, 62; in vocational education, 94

division of labor, based on gender in health care, 49

dominance, 145-146

Durant, Henry, 7

economic systems: and power, 78-79; and values, 155-156

education: and change, 28-29; compulsory, 62; defined, 4; and the human interest, 28-29; on legal rights and responsibilities, 112; male-defined, 7; as politics, 28; validity of, 3; of U.S. president and public officials, 112; vocational, 94; wholistic, 14

Eisler, Riane, 138

eligibility in HR 9030: for emergency assistance, 91; for public assistance, 88; for subsidized work and training, 82-83

employment: concept of in HR 9030, 101; of disabled, 86; and job search, 89; of minorities, 85; part-time, 88; of poor, 85; of women, 85

empowerment, via education, 28-29

environments, safe work, 106-107

Ephron, Nora, 7

ethics: feminist, 8; and genetics, 43; and leadership, 58; and population choices, 63

Equal Educational Opportunity Title IX of Education Amendments, 107

Equal Employment Opportunity Commission (EEOC): and health policy, 44; and NOW media task force, 123-124; Reagan funding cuts for, 140; violation by AT&T, 67

Equal Rights Amendment: effects of, 64, 114-115; and organization of health care, 37; support for, 138-139

equality principle, 80, 90

Face the Feminists, 129-132

Fairness Doctrine, of Federal Communications law, 120-121

family: concept of in HR 9030, 100; patriarchal definition of, 89; power in, 78

feasibility/simulation projects, for future searchers, 62-70

Federal Communications Commission (FCC): and affirmative action, 122-124; Fairness Doctrine of, 120

feeding, of infants, 45-46

femaleness, as biological trait, 12

feminine: introduction to concept, 11-13; see also entire book

feminine mystique, sustaining war, 137

feminism: introduction to concept, 8-9; see also entire book

feminist/gynandrous language, 13

feminist institutes, creation of, 68-69

feminist scholars, 15

feminist scholarship, 56-57

feminist studies: in existing institutions, 68-69; for health care providers, 49

feminist transcendent language, 11-13

feminist values, 143-146; and health care, 35-36, 48

Feminist Women for Peace, 74

First International Feminist Planning Conference, 46

food, women's role in production, 26

Food and Drug Administration (FDA), and DES, 42

food stamps, Reagan funding cuts in, 142

foreign affairs, and women, 150

funding: for abortion, 99; of corporations, 67; of future search, 64; of genetic research, 43; of health care, 44; of political campaigns, 113; sexism in, 64; for student aid programs, 107; of women's conferences, 152-153; see also budgets

future: studies of, 65-66; and values, 137

future search, 57-62; defined, 55; as dramatization, 68; feasibility/simulation projects for, 62-70; funding for, 64; of institutions, 65-67; of law, 63; for well-fare, 105-115

gender gap, 138-142; and Reagan and company, 140-142

gendering of knowledge, 8, 16-29

genetics: gendering of knowledge in, 22-23; research in, 43

genital mutilation, 45

Gilligan, Carol, 144-145

Gilligan, John, 25

Ginsberg, Eli, 67

Goldstein, Joan, 41

Gould, Carol, 19

gynandry, 11; defined, 119; and study of leadership, 58

Hacker, Sally, 27, 67

Harvard Semi-versity, 8, 26

head of household, meaning of term, 78-79

health: factors influencing, 35-36, 48; industrial, 44; mental, 40-41

health care, 33-54; and civil rights, 44; and consciousness, 40-47; definition of, 35-36; dehierarchilization of, 48; and demystification of knowledge, 37-38; deprofiteering of, 35; desexigration of, 49-50; and feminist values, 36; financing of, 44; instrumental approach to, 35-36; international, 44-46, 157; language of, 49; organization of, 37-38; reformulations of, 47-50; self-help movements in, 38-39; and sexism, 33, 45

homophobia, and sexism, 6

Hooks, Benjamin, 124
Hosken, Fran P., 45
housework, pay for, 78
HR 9030, 73-103, 105-116; cost effectiveness of, 101; traits of drafters of, 86; sexist language of, 79-81
human interest: communication in, 128; and education, 28-29; scholarship in. 55-72
humane, definition of, 109
humanity: via higher education, 1-32; quest for, 4-5
humanities, and wel-fare re-form, 109-110
humanization, of science, 20-21
hunger: and agribusiness, 25; and corporate malpractice, 42-43; in girls and boys, 42-43; proposed TV documentation of, 130; and social status, 26

illegal affirmative inaction, 92-100
illiteracy: social, 6, 112; of women and girls, 108-139
imagination, see poverty of imagination
imperialism, cultural, 45
impotence, 143
institutionalized practices, and oppression, 9, 99
instrumental approach to health care, 35-36
insurance, in financing health care, 44
integrity, 3, 8-9
international politics, 149-159
international health care, 44-46, 157
international issues: and feminist values, 155; and women, 150
International Tribunal on Crimes against Women, 46
International Women's Year Conference, Mexico, 44-45
International Women's Conference and Forum, Denmark, 158
International Women's Decade, 44-45
intrauterine device (IUD), 41
involuntary servitude: of compulsory pregnancy, 100; of compulsory school attendance for girls, 62; and HR 9030 provisions, 88

Jacklin, Carol, 24
jobs: assistance eligibility for, 83; discrimination in opportunities for, 95-96; in HR 9030, 101; matching, 96-97; number of, 89; part-time, 88; sharing, 113-114
jockstrap, emotional, 48
justice: in agribusiness, 27; and law, 63

Kahn, Herman, 65, 136
Kennedy, Florynce, 7
KNOW, Inc., 124-125
knowledge: and action, 70; demystification of, 37-38; compartmentalizing of, 9; degendering of, 9; and feminist scholarship, 57; gatekeepers of, 8; gendering of, 8, 16-29; and reproductive choice, 46-47
Kohlberg, Lawrence, 18

Lanham Act, 87
language, 10-13, 75-84; adversarial, 31n; and behavior, 11; as change agency, 118-120; and communication, 117; feminine terms in, 13; feminist transcendent, 11, 13; gynandrous, 13; in health care, 49; and laws, 62; male imagery of, 10-11, 79; masculine terms in, 13; of poverty, 75-81; polarization in, 11; and rape, 10; transcendent, 13; and values, 11
law: adversarial, 63, 131; enforcement of, 44, 61-62; feminist approaches to, 63; sexist language in, 62
leadership: BFOQ for, 58; and feminist scholarship, 57-58; and male-oriented values, 156; and nurturance, 58; and women's conferences, 156
learning, and behavior, 146
legislation, future search of, 67; for survival assistance, 84-86
lesbianism, 59-60
love, power of, 146

machismo, and international health, 154
Macoby, Eleanor, 24
male-oriented values, and leadership, 156
maleness, as biological trait, 11-12
malpractice: corporate, 130, 133n; drug, 41-42
mandamus action: defined, 44; for law enforcement, 95
manglish, 80, 118; of World Future Society, 137
Marieskind, Helen, 37-38
masculine: introduction to concept, 11-13; and feminine dualities, 16-17
masculine mystique, expressed in war, 137
masculinist ideology, 136-138
matriot, 71, 119
McNamara, Robert, 66
M.D.eity, 35
media, 120-127; Bakke case treatment, 125-126; discrimination in, 122-124; Houston conference coverage, 126-127; peace and, 121; and values, 109
Medicaid, funding for abortion, 99
medical model, 35
men, exclusion at women's conferences, 150-152
Mendelsohn, Everett, 20-21
mental health: double standard of, 40-41; proposed TV documentation on, 130
militarism, future search of, 59; as irrational, 146
Miller, Jean Baker, 47-48; 70, 145, 151
misogyny: and female health, 45; and gendering of knowledge, 17; and sexuality, 59-60; in sociobiology, 23
Moynihan, Daniel Patrick, 67
Myrdal, Alva, 59

National Endowment for the Humanities (NEH), 109-110
National Institute of Health (NIH), 40
National Institute of Mental Health (NIMH), 41

National Organization for Women (NOW): action in health care, 39; and CSDI, 65; and FCC action, 122-124; and First International Planning Conference, 46
National Peace Academy: breastimony on, 128-129; proposed TV coverage of, 130
National Women's Conference, Houston: assessment of, 158; on employment, 93-94; media coverage of, 126-127; on welfare and poverty, 93; on women and business, 114
National Women's Health Network, 39
National Women's Political Caucus, 98
Nestle Corporation, 46
Network on the New Reproductive Technologies, 43
news, rating of top stories, 126
NOW Legal Defense and Education Fund (NOW-LDEF), 40, 107
Nurses' Coalition for Action in Politics (N-CAP), 39
Nurses NOW, 39, 52n
nursing: definition of, 33; politicizing of, 39; role in health care, 34
nurturance: assertive, 38, 51, 145; of change agents, 71; and leadership, 58; and international policy, 157; and health care, 33

obedience to conscience, 132
objectivity: and pseudo-objectivity, 4; in science, 20
Occupational Safety and Health Administration (OSHA), 106-107
old husband's tales, about war-fare, 106
oppression: designers for change of, 152; via institutionalized practices, 9, 99; and sexism, 6
ourstory, defined, 119

passion, 71
patriarchy: and agribusiness, 27; and conflict of interest, 117; inhumane consequences of, 154; and militarism, 59
peace: and conflict resolution, 127-129; as feminist values transformation, 143; as 59; as rational yearning, 145-146
philosophy: feminism as, 8; gendering of knowledge in, 19
physicians, role in health care, 34-36
Piercy, Marge, 34
police work, future search of, 61-62
policy: in financing health care, 44; international, 155-156; and peace, 59; reformulation in health care, 48, 157; and values, 145; women's participation in making, 40, 150
politics: of education, 28; and genetic research, 43; international, 149-159; of rape, 2; sexism and, 39
political activism, in health care, 39
population choices: future search of, 62-63; proposed TV portrayal of, 130; reproductive choice and, 46-47; and World Bank, 66
post-feminism, 70

poverty: language of, 75-81; and National Women's Conference, Houston, 93; and public welfare crisis, 77; victims of, 84; and World Bank, 66
poverty of imagination, 74-75, 112, 113
power: in communication, 117; economic, 78-79; of genetics, 23; in health care system, 35; and leadership, 57; love of, 146; in nuclear family, 78; and patriarchy, 154; redefined in health care, 46, 48-49; redefined through communications, 120; and self-help, 38
pregnancy, compulsory, 46-47, 100
print media, 124-127
Project on Equal Education Rights (PEER), 107
psychosurgery, 40-41

race, race-IQ debate, 23
racism, and sexism, 6, 30n, 60, 156
Radcliffe, 8
radical, defined, 153; feminism, 64
radicalism, as common sense, 153
rape: definition of, 3; educational, 3; of human consciousness, 9; intellectual, 3, 6; via language, 10; physical, 2; as political act, 2
Raymond, Janice, 43
Reagan and company, 46, 74, 115n, 140-142
re-form, of wel-fare, 110-115
reproductive choice, 46-47; see also population choice
re-search: in agribusiness, 26; defined, 57; funding of, 32n, 43; in genetics, 43; see also future search
Restore Our Alientated Rights (ROAR), 60
Rich, Adrienne, 17, 135
Robins, A.H. Co., 41
Russell, Michelle, 14-15

Sangamon State, 14
scholarship, 55-72; androcentric, 55; feminist perspectives on, 56-57; and leadership, 57-58; traditional, 57, 67
scholarship/activism: in collaboration, 70-71; see also activism/thought
science: and change, 50; definition of, 20; gendering of knowledge in, 20-22; and feminism, 22, 50-51; objectivity in, 20

Sangamon State, 14
scholarship, 55-72; androcentric, 55; feminist perspectives on, 56-57; and leadership, 57-58; traditional, 57, 67
scholarship/activism: in collaboration, 70-71; see also activism/thought
science: and change, 50; definition of, 20; gendering of knowledge in, 20-22; and feminism, 22, 50-51; objectivity in, 20

Seaman, Barbara, 37
security, definitions of, 139-140
self-help, in health care, 38-39
seminal, defined, 19
semi-versities, 6-9; defined, 4
Sex Bias in the U.S. Code, 80, 102n
sex differences, sociobiological study of, 24-25

sex discrimination, *see* discrimination; *see also* sexism
sex similarities, in behavior, 24
sexism: and agribusiness, 27; in funding, 64; in health care, 33, 45; institutionalization of, 99; in law, 62; as oppression, 6; in politics, 39; and racism, 30n, 60-61, 156; and reproductive knowledge, 46-47; and scholarship, 56
sexuality, 59-60
shero, 118
Sipila, Helvi, 154
Small Business Administration, 114, 116n
social illiteracy: of existing civil rights, 112; in higher education, 4, 6
socialization: and gender gap, 139; and health, 36; and humaneness, 109; and leadership, 57; and sex stereotyping, 145-146
sociobiology, gendering of knowledge in, 23-25
sociology, gendering of knowledge in, 18-19
specialization: in health care, 37-38, 49; in scholarship, 57
Stanton, Elizabeth Cady, 30n
Strick, Anne, 63
subjectivity, 4, 20
survival assistance: defined, 77; and education, 107-108; legislation proposed for, 84-86
Sweden, 59, 143

technical assistance for women, 114-115
technocracy, and reproductive choice, 47
technology, and health care, 35-36
television: critical incident studies of, 68; discrimination in programming, 122-124; dramatization of poverty realities, 110; Face the Feminists, 126-132
tenure, academic, 12, 58-59
terminal testosterone poisoning, 70
testimony, defined, 73; *see also* breastimony
third world, and agribusiness, 25
thought and activism, in collaboration, 50-51
Toffler, Alvin, 66
transcendence, feminist, 8-9
transcendent language, 13

United Nations International Women's Decade, 44-45
University of Massachusetts, 43
U.S. Code, 80

validity, of scientific knowledge, 20
values: and academic tenure, 58-59; in budgets, 141-142; and economic systems, 155-156, and future, 136-137; and gender gap, 138-139; in health care, 35-36, 48; and international policy, 155; in language, 11; masculine, 136; and media, 109; and peace, 143-146; and public policy, 145; and scholarship, 56-57; and science, 50-51

values transformation, 8, 143-146
victim, blaming of, 7

war: as consequence of masculinism, 136-138; as impotence to resolve conflict, 143
war-fare, 106
wealth, control of, 139
welfare: cash assistance programs of H.R. 9030, 91; defined, 75-76, 78; distribution of, 77; for military men, 98; reform, 77, 110-115; resources redirected to, 106-110; *see also* survival assistance
Wellesley College, 2-3, 7, 12
wholeness, of education, 8-9; 28-29
wholism, and health care, 34
Wildavsky, Aaron, 35
Window Dressing on the Set, 122-123
womb envy, 43
women: as consultants, 95; as leaders, 156; literacy of, 108; portrayal by media, 121-122; *see also* entire book
Women, Infants and Children Food Program (WIC), Reagan funding cuts for, 142
Women's Bureau, Reagan funding cuts for, 140
women's conferences: exclusion of men from, 150-152; funding of, 152-153; on international issues, 150-157; leadership of, 156; radical perspectives and, 153; representativeness of, 152-153
women's health movement, and self-help, 38-39
Women's International League for Peace and Freedom (WILPF), 138
women's issues, defined, 129-130, 154
women's studies: as affirmative action, 12-16; and art, 15-16; for health care providers, 49; as degree requirement, 4
women's university, 69
words: creation of, 118-119; *see also* language
work: concept of in H.R. 9030, 101; safe environments for, 106-107
World Agricultural Research Project, 26-27
World Bank, 66
World Future Society (WFS), 65-66, 137, 147n